SHADE 2004

SHADE 2004

DAVID DODD LEE,
EDITOR

MARGARET VON STEINEN,
ASSISTANT EDITOR

Four Way Books
New York City

Distributed by
University Press of New England
Hanover and London

Editorial Office
Four Way Books
POB 535, Village Station
New York, NY 10014
www.fourwaybooks.com

Library of Congress Catalogue Card Number: 2002116851

ISBN 1-884800-50-5

Four Way Books is a division of Friends of Writers, Inc., a Vermont-based not-for-profit organization. We are grateful for the assistance we receive from individual donors and private foundations.

Distributed by University Press of New England
One Court Street, Lebanon, NH 03766

This book is manufactured in the United States of America and printed on acid-free paper.

CONTENTS

SHADE 2004

Check-In

I'm just calling to check in.
Do I still have to check in?
Maybe this time I'll scoot past the manager,
Slip a five to the Dick
In the phone booth,
Stick a fat book in the fire door.

Or I'll sign a lease on a six-room apartment.
I'll buy a house that overlooks the Hudson.
Mort and the guys
Are coming over Tuesday
To pour a foundation for the outdoor patio.
Better watch your step.

I've been missing you all of these hours.
My love for you is red-hot.
That span between "Hey" and "Good-bye"
Was an elm tree
Burned to an ash-heap,
A sign blinking open and opening.

My love for you is the hotel register
Opened to the thirtieth page
Swimming with brown and blue ink.
My love for you is an overheated pool
And a swollen movie magazine.
My love for you is five o'clock in the morning.

My love for you is five o'clock
In the morning, two sheets
Of paper crumpled at the bottom of the can.
Someone left a bathing suit on the hook.
The air conditioner is turned up to High.
A car is pulling away from a door left wide open.

Angel Eyes

You, who yanked my hair back until I cried out more
Because I thought you'd like it, as I did, in a sense,
You behind me, gasping *My angel, it's heaven, I adore*

You. Leaves turning slowly towards the forest floor.
We tried first on a rock, autumnal, immense
But you pressed me to bark and I cried out for more.

I've thought it over, and there is no cure
For elbowing sunlight, the swallow and silence
That follows, slams in the wind like a door.

'Scuse me while I disappear. You pour
Coffee and stir, *A fine romance*
With no quarrels, and no insults, and all morals—

I crashed the car—drove in straight up the sore
Underside of a Buick. Glass showered our pants
As passers-by pulled and beat at the door.

Baby, I've got news for you—I'm from Missouri
Too, croons the windshield. Patience,
Angel. Pass the plate and holler for more
And beat like a drum on the door, on the door.

Tenants

Before she knew everything
There was to know, in May,

He moved her to the cabin
Beside the lake. A gray

Rose from the bottom
Like mist, into the tracks

Of a thousand tenants
And their departing backs.

Like a recording of which
She was particularly fond,

She thought again of the wet
Mop, salamander, the pond

Scum rising like fur
From the bones underneath.

In December, voices clattered
Like her chattering teeth.

How did you stop their chattering?
She sank beneath

Her quilt. He said
What's this? She said

What's what? Enough,
He said, *Get out of bed.*

Before, she thought
—her teeth kept chattering—

There was this *this*
There was this everything.

Wild Kingdom

The family is thought of in anthropological terms:
That strange tribe with their strange customs.
Dinner at nine. The laundry
on the floor. Clocks
always, always, set to different times.

There is an older Bear, the largest
Bear, with hair the color of a chimney.
Smoke comes out of his eyes.
Smoke comes out of his ears.
There is never enough porridge.

The Monkey waits in the tree.
Water hardens on her face.
She hides her teeth behind her hands
And nods her head
Up up up up up.
Then she stops
To talk to all the neighbors.

(The neighbors' clothes
Are cut from crinoline and their faces
Carved from Ivory bars.
Everything about them is clean.
The hands are
Clean. The mattresses
Are clean. The dimples are clean.)

Where are the littlest Bears?
The oldest one is telling jokes.
Why does God have such little hands?
Wee paws. That's one joke, split in two.
For station identification—
God thinks he's Nelson Rockefeller, today.

This oldest Bear gets
Most Unobserved.
He waits upstairs
With his geodes, spaceships, and rubber-bands.

This youngest Bear
Is yellow and cuddly.
She gets Most Butter Face.
She goes wee wee wee
from 9 a.m. to 3:15.
She is the Monkey's afterthought.

This middle bear waits in the grass.
Baa, baa, black sheep—
Have you any wool?
A headful.
She gets
Most Kissed. She
Is anybody's anything.

Tyringham, 1998

After Horace

It had always been my dream during that time
  To create a contraceptive line
For females—"During"—
  Shelved like Pantene Pro-V shampooing,
By kind: Nonoxynol-9–
  Free & with, K-Y, self-fitting di-
aphragm kits, spermicide buffered with enzyme,

And the morning-after pill—the girl's grand Grand Trine—
  Ortho Tri-Cyclen in triplicate.
We're in the country.
  The bottoms of my feet are filthy,
The fridge is sown with mouse shit
  But somehow I am heedless: I buy
A week's worth of carrots and serve them with wine.

An astrologer said I had a Grand Trine
  In the right-hand corner of my chart:
I can't sink too low.
  Where are diaphragms designed to go?
I ask you, my knees apart.
  Under the radiator—a joke
Of my mother's. Aeronautical design.

Mine slips in like a thief. Behind, from the ass,
  You hardly feel the circle curving;
Up on my belly
  A seeping tread of slickened jelly
Betrays the sheets. I'm bringing
  Forth wine for famine, a noonday fast
Of spermatozoa and freshly mown grass.

Mt. Desert Island

I had an experiment to gauge the pitch of snails humming.
My love was Ricky: marine biologist, mole on the right cheek.
His girlfriend ran every morning.
The Iranian and I argued in the minivan
And I told the lesbian, "I'm not a lesbian.
A woman's leg is art." She was Republican;
I drank Chablis in her 4 x 6 room.
I was fourteen. One of the girls
Had 1600s on her S.A.T.'s;
Another 800 in math. They weighed
Us one by one—"You'll need a large"—
And I was in love with the suit.
I was in love with the waves
And the motorboat's hum. On a visit
My father took me for nouvelle cuisine.
My duck was aged: "That's not enough."
The beige, fin-de-siècle suit
From the corner antique's:
"You've got enough already."
We caught dogfish. We dissected
Dogfish. We caught snails
While crabs scuttled in their tidal pools.
Madame, I would like to fuck you. No matter.
I am abhorred by a Canuck, embraced
By a Canadienne. I slept watching the shore,
Waiting for the Dramamine to kick in.
I could not train my eyes on the horizon.
They took us to Mt. Snow
To see the constellations,
Where the Iranian
Biked every Sunday.
I lay with the lesbian
(a mystical experience).
And she told me the sequence:
Girls' Hockey, split tendon.

Was she really a lesbian?
When we traced summer graves
Out on Cranberry Island
The red spread like wine
On the dark, sleeping waves.

Grand Central, Track 23

I forgot to tell you it's almost time to go.
The sun has distilled its particular worn essence
And the glittering trout is flipped on the bow.

A man asks me what time it is. I don't know.
I have emptied my purse and wept in the presence
Of onlookers. I forgot to remember to go

Before eleven, when the steely arrow
Shot swimming to its underneath, tense
As a stream of salmon in reverse below

The laureled, relentless clocks. The sceptered row
Of columns dreams one o'clock, immense,
Inviolate. What time is it? I don't know.

This story concerns the night I tried to go—
Though many times I flopped into the silence
Of orange plastic seating like trout onto the bow

Of a lonely ship, and felt my breathing slow.
The frail, retreating stand of columns prevents
The clocks from telling me time and again to go.
At my feet, a glittering trout swims past the bow.

Grief

First, it will comfort you to know there are crows.
And calipers for measuring the amount of sunshine
that can escape from under the shadows
of thought. Far out at sea ships go down
in a crippled light, and bunches of black iris
are sent to the remaining crew.
You, too, shall have lived and died
a jot, with the queer feeling you were vast and
ageless, with a good education in sleep, prepared
to die with one regret, that you could not devote
more years in vain. And no one could do nothing
but let it happen. Whatever was tied to the mast
the waves have come—here they are:
after anxiety turns into pain and pain
turns into rain and the rain
into a doorbell on the face,
the forehead splits open.
Crows come for that speck of gold
you were saving for your eyelids at the point of death
and turn away, wildly happy.

Sweet Morning

They lined up all the Psalms,
all one hundred and fifty of them,
and shot them one by one.

They threw them in a trench
made for the purpose of burying Psalms.

And did the Psalms rise up,
did they rise up singing?

Did the Psalms stay together,
did the Psalms disperse?

Did the twenty-third Psalm escape,
and come to your house
and ask for a ride?

Imagine you are the belated passenger.
Tell what happened to you and what you saw.

I saw one hundred and fifty bathers
come to a wide, calm lake
at the end of a long, hot day.

I saw one hundred and fifty bathers
take off their clothes and swim slowly
to the other side, with a long cool joy
like that of swans and dogs.

How do you explain this?

By way of the oft-repeated.
By way of sorrow's root.
By way of the swinging lantern.
And by the face of stars
drowning in the morning light.

Statement

I used to write obituaries for the Cleveland Press in the summer, when nobody died. Nobody ever died in the summer, or hardly anybody, maybe one or two in the middle of July or something, but in general it wasn't a good time to be having a death watch. It was boring, that's all, and I began to use the names of births for the obits, I mean I used the baby's names, there were plenty of them, the summer was a good time to be born, absolutely loaded with births, so I thought why not, no one will notice, or if they did notice it would be in a pleasant way, a touch of surprise that things were at long last leveling out. Maybe one or two might raise an eyebrow and wonder what it meant to have an unusually high number of babies go from the maternity ward straight to the morgue, but it wasn't like I was killing them or anything, I was just a reporter doing my job, and you know there are more people than you might suppose who read the obituaries regularly, if not religiously, and I got a certain amount of satisfaction in keeping them happy, why not, without that it would have been an even crappier job than it was, especially in the summer, when things were as I have said, slow, if not at a standstill. That's all. One of those two keen readers noticed and there was a ruckus and I was fired. I lost my job. I paid for my mistake, but believe me it wasn't a joke, it was never a joke, and today I no longer even feel it was a mistake, I feel that for one brief shining moment the number of people born equaled the number of people who died, those who came in went out, and life in Cleveland that summer was fair.

Kiss of the Sun

If, as they say, poetry is a sign of something
among people, then let this be prearranged now,
between us, while we are still peoples: that
at the end of time, which is also the end of poetry
(and wheat and evil and insects and love),
when the entire human race gathers in the flesh,
reconstituted down to the infant's tiniest fold
and littlest nail, I will be standing at the edge
of that fathomless crowd with an orange for you,
reconstituted down to its innermost seed protected
by white thread, in case you are thirsty, which
does not at this time seem like such a wild guess,
and though there will be no poetry between us then,
at the end of time, the geese all gone with the seas,
I hope you will take it, and remember on earth
I did not know how to touch it it was all so raw,
and if by chance there is no edge to the crowd
or anything else so that I am of it,
I will take the orange and toss it as high as I can.

The Feather

Helping sister rearrange her china cabinet,
watching her parakeet die: those were the days.
In full power of our lives we were endlessly rearranging
everything in our paths, but not immune to the pain
of others. We had a balance going there for awhile,
one of us on tiptoe while the other held the plate.
Then the crash, followed by Oscar's Olympic attempt
to drag himself up using his beak as a claw,
then the almost bare sound of a feather
making its way down, taking its time,
almost enjoying this day of dogged perfection
when we were all lumped together in the house,
and wafting on about the wars that were fought
so it might have this moment of leisure.

The Terror of Transience

The night is stone
The tears of fireflies cannot dent it

and the whores running through the grasses
cannot catch the fireflies

and the sleepwalker stopping by the waterfall
wakes suddenly and does not hear his heart

No one in all the night understands the train schedule
or the event that stripped the geraniums of their reds

and on the shore snails die
leaving their bodies behind
which will last forever

The Water Table

Harold's 15-year-old daughter
knew about two safeties
and unlocked them
but didn't know about
the third—a
hidden pin—
and couldn't get the
gun to fire. Harold's
blue-eyed, intense
daughter who now lives
in California,
23, with 7 years sobriety.
You can tell he
doesn't want to let her
go back, but
how can he hold her, only 4
years sober
himself? The water
of life,
Father John says, cleans
us, heals us;
we are dipped down in
it, allowed
to die, and then
brought back up
without that original
sin that
makes us so unpleasant.
Devil,
get thee behind me.
The water has
to be alive, moving,
hence the pond

Monsignor Regan had dredged
behind the rectory
for baptisms 20 years
ago. Now,
retired, he dips in
and out of
the hospital, out of
lucidity, but perfectly
clear, he gushes,
"You and
your husband have
so much
and those girls . . . .
He said he
wants a divorce?" Then,
with a laugh,
"Those are only
words." Each
time I see him, I drink
him up, afraid I'll soon be
left with his
New Testament
translated by Knox
and my spotty
memory. Harold says when
Jessica goes back
to California, she'll
start again at college,
aim for something
to do with
emergency medicine,
and I remember
what Ann said, that
emergency work is
a typical career
choice of "children
from dysfunctional

families." She
told me about a man who's gone so
far as to become
a salvage diver, an
underwater
EMT; we laughed,
thinking of Freud
and the great unconscious,
to be able
to swim in it
every day, and
save people. Jessica
could save anyone,
I think—she saved
me a few
weeks ago when
I thought
I would sink, my
marriage set
adrift on the
great
change of life—I can't
believe they call
it that. Does every woman
fall asleep and
wake back up in
a different life?

Every week
for two weeks now
Father John
has prayed for
the teenage lovers, Andrea
and Jeff, who
died in a stall
in the Ladies Room
at Central High. He prays,

his voice
breaking as though he
too would break. And we
picture them
curled there. Not as
they were—the janitor
who found them,
after all, had
to be
hospitalized afterward, but as
we'd like them
to be, two babes
in the wood
who lay down in
a grassy glade
and didn't get back
up.
We come out from mass,
this is Georgia,
January 17,
to a
spring rain. John,
my brother,
tells us at dinner
that what
will get us in the end
will be
the water table—all those
pesticides
have to eventually
go somewhere,
that pesky original
sin, like
the Cat in the Hat's
pink bath-
tub ring.
Somewhere

awaits the savior
    or little
cat "Z"
    who, in one
decisive blow, one
    electric jolt, one
ZOOM, will
    clean it up.
                I
saw a painting called
    The Fifth Step
once, a black velvet background
    with paint
squiggles and other detritus
    all over it, the great
unconscious unburdening
    itself—
the guy who painted
    it went
back out. I saw him
    at a coffee
shop one day, flushed
    and shaking, faking
it. Carl, I think his
    name was,
and I haven't thought of
    him in years.
He wore white painter's pants
    and was so
intent and charming in
    meetings. I didn't
fall in love with him,
    though. I was
a thousand per cent in
    love with my
husband; there was
    a kind of harmony

then, my sins were fitting
in well,
I guess, in a way
they simply
aren't now. Money
& children &
mortgages hadn't raised
their heads.
Hot flashes, car
wrecks, marriage
counseling and carpenter
bees, killer wisteria,
runaway ivy and the ten
deep, muddy
holes Sally has dug
in the
backyard. Mammogram
callbacks, bone density
studies, and borderline
ovarian function,
St. John's Wort, memory
enhancement
pills and the 5-foot
laundry tower. Sheila's
bone marrow transplant and
subsequent graft vs.
host disease. Inappropriate
crushes on
gas station
attendants,
convenience store
clerks, sweaty intramural
basketball players
at the gym. God, Jesus,
Mary, and all
the saints,
I can't carry this

mess, *my*
mess any longer,
dip me
down in that sprinkler,
hose, puddle, whatever's
handy, that I might
be cleaned, that
we might be
cleaned,
healed of our
bitter resentments,
our *spiritual pride,*
our *doubt, distress,*
our *fear of death*, that
we might be
healed of our
messy
trespasses.

Part of the Forest

The red poppies on the paper fan mirror
the blush of the girl's sweater. She turns away;
we don't understand her face. We only know
that somewhere in the painting she is alone,
looking toward a darkness beyond us.

It's the devil you would like to extinguish.
The one that is hiding in the still life between
the bright yellow pear and the claw of a bird.
It makes the painting deteriorate before it's finished.

The baroque angels are sinking on top of you.
Lower. And the temperature drops. Your mouth
is a wrinkled heart, twice deflated, ear pressed
to the floor. Sexless, you are more like a peach,
praying in the damp cold, haze coming from your mouth.

Someone is laughing next door. The bell rings.
You put your arms around the messenger,
make love to him by the doorway.
A flower appears in the hollow space
you carved with your silence and regret.

The sky dims like a painting, a scene where you wish
you were living. It's the hands that do the work.
The devil pushes the girl's hair behind her small ear.
You can hear his music. You might know the song.
The words in your mouth taste like sugar, gun powder.

Lencois

If I go to sleep will I hear the stars behind me,
the flecks of malcontent forming like bruises,
the universe gone purple in my purple quarters.

I see everything ahead of me, a long stretch of
dry pale road or maybe a city that will soon be
submerged in water, where the women walk

balancing pots on their heads as if they themselves
were balancing on the edge of the world.
And if in my sleep, I arrive in Brazil, will you

walk with me along the banks of Lencois,
where the women wash their beautiful backs
unembarrassed as if they were washing their pots,

their rags. Their bodies bare and open
as they thrash a wet dress along the flat rocks.
The whole world is bleached now,

gone with a translucent stain that I cannot
wash off my hands. And if I walk further
will I see the remains of what the butcher has laid out,

the head of a bull, open eyes staring.
Right ear cut off. The curve of it lying
in the dirt. The butcher laughs.

Unreal light on the dark animal, black eyes
searing the bright world. If I choose to ignore it,
will I stumble through the open market, past a pile

of children's shoes for sale, disheveled heaps
of white shoes like stones, their soles
turned upside down.

The Burning

> *"...I've lived without names..."*
> *– Stephen Kuusisto*

Off a seashore in Russia I run, laughing
at the mystery of movement in the form
of water, laughing at my father with sand
on his face who will one day die.

Or imagine for a minute a locomotive
full of people, rocking with the motion
of a vintage sorrow, head bowing as if
time has beaten them. In my winter season

I think of monks in Penang who sit without
sound for weeks. How they live inside silence.
The silence is alive. The ringing of a bell
is an intricate acorn; my soul hits the ground

when it falls. The apple for all its perfection
will never change. The seed I swallow fashions
a knot in my throat, the fiber of the peel winds
like a staircase leading me down. I look

at my teeth-marks in fruit, in flesh
like a message, an erotic code deciphered
by tearing & biting down. I want to keep
this braille, this transcript of my soul:

My body is a vessel of wanting.
My body is a vessel of fury.
My body is a vessel of apology.

I am the thread & the damage the thread made after the mending.

I am a black tree blown sideways & the fire that burns with no fuel.

three poems from

Reassembling the Bodily Relics of St. Gemma Galgani (Italy, 1878-1903)

Letter from Eufemia Giannini to Palmira Valentini Written in the Last Mortal Hours of Gemma Galgani

Lucca, 1903

The Lord winked when He left
the Devil in this room. Winked, walked out,
and never returned. Frightened for Gemma,
we brought in Christ's face,
ran the wall through with nails
and hung Him before her.
Air hangs here as usual,
but there's no comfort in it –
no angel, no Jesus, no mother
of God. She complains we don't empty
her bed fast enough: that scorpions, snakes
slip in and bite her; that trash we can't see
must be thrown out the window.
She always was her own fire,
now she's the fuel
consuming herself. Well water,
holy water—nothing exists wet enough
to extinguish this fever,
to wash what we can't see from her sight.

One rare night she slept
I doused all the candles,
prayed for some glow off her body
to throw off the dark.
But that black only deepened,

thickened, then ground
down on her breathing,
on her ragged, blood-soaked breath.
What had I done? Not God,
but kerosene, tallow
finally restrained it,
reined that darkness back in.
If it weren't for Satan,
the most mundane of deaths
would be keeping me company.
But even the Devil must sleep.
Just for those moments,
Gemma's only a girl,
almost a sister.
Three years I knelt
entranced before her—
the body, the blood—
On my aunt's bedroom floor
her soft skin offered, opened for Jesus
while I watched her watching God. That girl,
who wouldn't so much as look
in a mirror, but whose prayers
held the voice of a woman
alone in her room,
touching herself into her lover's arms.

Palmira, forgive me,
but may Christ never come back
to suffer in her skin –
She has no strength to support Him.
Tell me, how will we learn
to live with her dead,
with the priests
who'll come to bury her Jesus
in the taste of dry bread
they'll so publicly place on our tongues?

Last Letter of Giulia Galgani
Sent to Her Sister, Gemma Galgani

Cerreto di Sopra, 1902

Gemma, I'm dying. And why not?
It's the one thing our family
seems to be good at. Father,
Mother, Carlo, Gino—Remember
how Jesus once told you, *Daughter,*
you are not made for this world?
Well, maybe all the Galganis
weren't meant for this earth.

What makes you so jealous
you won't come see me?
Christ taking me first although
I don't want Him? What bothers you most
is I'd rather a husband,
a *casa*, an infant, a respectable
life. But now it's no matter. I'm eighteen,
tubercular—nobody's prospect.
My sister called crazy all over town.
Gemma, you've no idea
the gossip that swallows us,

what it is
to walk out the door, knowing
these are my choices: to be looked at with pity
or not looked at at all. The word falls

from windows: *contagious,*
contagious,

meaning: *How long till Giulia starts acting like Gemma?*
meaning: *How long till that girl becomes a hysteric?*

I stopped wearing gloves in the winter
so everyone sees that my palms aren't split open,

that my hands don't tear open like yours.

Let the Lord Jesus keep His wounds to Himself.

Once blood was a word,
always written in black,
now it's a red I can barely

stop saying. A thread I hang onto –
worn through, frayed, but still durable

enough to obligate: our rich aunt
takes me in so I'll die

in a bed,
not on the floor near a plate of gnawed bones.

Each night, brother walks here from Lucca,
signs the shadow of the cross
over my face. You know his health –
In a month, maybe two, Tonino will join me.
We'll lie down together in that part
of the cemetery marked *For the poor*
and wretched. A kind of family reunion –
more of us buried than walking the earth.

Gemma, the two of us talked and we ask you,
Don't come to us.
We don't know what to do

with inconceivable grief—Your sorrow,
not that we die, not that we leave you,
but that God wants to keep you
in this world.

The Sworn Deposition of Angelina Galgani Concerning the Servant of God, Gemma Galgani

Ecclesiastical Proceedings, Lucca, 1922

Take it or leave it. I'm where
blood memory ends. *Least luminous member*
of the Galgani home. The only one in the family
not allergic to air, who didn't strangle
on her own lungs.

You think my sister a saint?
Her blood certainly oozed
in all the right places. No skinned knees,
surgery, razor to the wrist—Girl stripped
of all secular scars, girl too good
for mere secular wounds.

I used to swear just to watch her sweat blood.

I'd jam her keyhole with trash –
She couldn't lock me out. Whole days in the bedroom,
down on her knees, out of her head. Eyes locked
on the empty air. I'd stand between her
and God, but her eyes
worked through me, unblinking.
Pins, pinchings, a slap—Nothing
would wake her. Nothing done to Christ's pet
irked Him into existence.

It gave me strength to stop believing in God.

Medieval throwback. Freak of the family.
I threw open her windows,
Hey everyone, come see the ecstatic!
Hey boys and girls, come view a stigmata!
What the rest of us had
wasn't good enough for Gemma:

Prayer-life lasting the length of a rosary,
then pocketed once you were done.
My brothers would never admit
their *thrill* when she left
with the Gianninis: Pious busybodies
taking her in. What'd they think when their doctor
wiped down my sister, when they saw
a girl bleed without wounds?

She slept on a cot, less a guest
than a servant. Satan snatched all her writings
then brought them back scorched. That family
must have roasted each page
until it had blackened,
until it read like a library from Hell.

I bet they're kicking themselves
for burning her deathbed, for washing out towels
where she coughed up her lungs. Sure, I know the law
against selling her relics. But born of the same mother,
her blood is mine. The blood of your saint
dead ends in my body. Snake oil. Tonic.
I cut myself and her miracle
soaks into hankies. It's a bargain I'm selling
a few drops at a time.

To Danae

"Danae, in the promiscuities
of springtime I wish we

were as two zonked Ophelias
again—girls on Kawasakis—

having doffed our woolens,
parents & perspective,

we would ride on scooters
risen out of bogland

sweaterless, with or without
nipple-rings, our lips chapped,

in great gravity our thoughts
forgotten two seconds

after thinking, only
would you not

let your mood resemble
so much the phonetics

of your name, Danae?
in denial you make us

into two ants devoted
to moving a bowling ball,

but in acceptance a hybrid
glance would pass

between us, electrons
shifting orbit, parted mouths

the portals of many words,
happy histocompatible smooth.

In this way, tooling around,
no clap of stoned lightning

would strike us, no
sea kelp cold & lunar

could wash out the road
at Hixbridge Crossing,

no wind harm us, please
discard your sadness,

as you were taught by
the child you were,

who once refused forever
to eat tail of ox

soup or shellfish—
in those days the ecstasy

of your enemies
was weak, much weaker

than yours,
remember?"

Delightful Soup

Pulpwork & seed
in the sliced-open halves of
cantaloupe—
                    it makes
of the weekend a
sweet space
in which to be
bucktoothed & saddled
in the crossed-up
rain,
      this one
mood having fallen for
three days
on a tapping
aluminum ladder left misaligned
against aluminum
siding—
           but
let's face it,

after we have
scooped through orange to the green
of rind,

and the soup is on
and the sea boils,

at dark a woman
and man will swim themselves
stupid.

I know why,
      to be spellbound because
      their mother
      has died, the two

too poor to travel overland
to her funeral,

tho what
lie wasn't she
capable of
while alive?

You, you neighbors
of mine, I know
your business, you there

basting in your
angry juices,

but to be alive is to be
impatient,

and confronted by endless
questions any
mother is vulnerable.

If you need
to forgive, forgive her
now,

but don't
be dour about it;

otherwise,
I'd rather spit
in this soup
than shake your hands.

Suit Me

On Thursdays I wear pants other men have worn.
I say pants make the man.
I dally in my walk, no pen or memory to rescue
from loss. Because I've become my mother, I rifle
through evicted furniture. Something waits
to stab the finger. I dig, ruthless, shameful.
I, my father's impersonator, walk dangerously close
to undertaking an understanding.
I have misplaced my gender.
I love, for example, Mary Ruefle. Or June.
In men's undies I can own both loves, no?
Later, there will be a refrain: why are my keys
in your purse?
Watch for the emotional crawl. The female will speak.
Sidewalks idle dangerously close.
Here, tripping along sidewalks is not lyrical,
but loose. If I admit my gender
is in the garbage, what have I confessed?
Why can't, for example, a dumpster be home?
They will say: too off-center, or june, or
for the next four blocks humps scratch the road.
Unruly pollen reminds of loss and beginning.
Burnt leaves, we say. Or scorched. As if detached
hands dangle with lit matches. Remove,
quite purposefully, green. As I remove the dress.
A man backs his car, wants desperately to stop
me for directions. What are you? He might query.
If I stop for him, I lose everything.
Stop and chatter with the cat, as if he understands
meaning is homeless. Like gender.
I am no inquest!
Later, a refrain: why are my keys in a purse?

the dirthills

Chiggers attached to stomachs, crickets hanging
from careless heads. Exposed children,
no pubic hair and nubs for breasts. The day
I brought the Bible there was just enough.

Mike was Adam. Beth, Eve. Sean played Abel.
Kimmie, Cain. I was the designated God,
the forbidden fruit. My body had matured
faster than my mind, or my body chased

a mind trained to cover nudity like shame.
Like a Bible. We didn't read much Bible.
Whatever happened in the dirthills
would break us. It should have stormed; the wind

should have been fierce. God should have stopped us.
But I was the designated God that day.

The King Emperor

They say they sat on the moldy border near a kousa dogwood, under a different low-growing tree, which is the oldest tree in the story. It has arching branches, red berries and fine-textured, robust bark.

Both were commenting that there is always something each wishes for that comes true.

He took his neckerchief off and the gauntlets, and his soiled coat—touched it willingly on the sleeve—and fawned over the woman whose name is Beth Schwenk and I am not just blowing smoke up your ass. He said, "Oh, you have been everywhere!"

People—and I do too—present stories and stories about him just to destabilize.

He had the clamber to hump Schwenk and to enjoy what he frogged or was able to wring off as a prisoner of the love scene.

There is much impertinence in trying to make more of this public.

He's sure got a weak spot for her, but it's getting harder all of the time at the dirty end of his stick when his chances come to pass in reality.

Just to have a name like his name must be such a pleasure. He's had two chances. Now they hear him promising.

It sounds as if he's right around the corner now in all of June, even if he had to stand in the no-hope-for-you corridor.

He knows the collection of laws.

He has relief in The House decorated by Blue China Furs and semievergreen shrubs with poorly-stemmed flowers planted in well-drained soil. The House is equipped with tiles and portraits of people who see right through me. It's heartbreaking pretending to be sympathetic to him. He taught his horse to jump. Yes, he's voluptuous and kind and the eldest son of the first gentleman. Some of the most momentous daughters and sons come from that guy.

He is popular with the people, unplain in face and one of the great men with his plump heart so animadverted upon.

He wasn't as great as this before this rain. He will be hardly much different after the rain.

He took the candle and the blankets and is noisy and difficult because he's the fellow who lives with Beth Schwenk and what shoots forth from him he pledges is the light in his eyes. Schwenk waits for me.

I see what this is. I've screwed my head off in the middle of my neck for the royalty.

Limited resources

I'd like to but can't draw. I tape
sticks to construction paper
in the shape of whimsy. Some people
have faces like the zoo breeds
on the wrong side of bars, faces
trying to break out.
I draw these by chewing dirt.
Most of the people who look good
on paper are other people.
Most of the clever things said
never were. Like, did the idea
of the thought balloon come
in a thought balloon? I am
the person who never said that.
Years ago I was drawn
while sleeping on the sofa.
The woman who drew me
used forty eight lines.
I counted them before kissing
her fingers. She said who I am
with economy and by smearing
pencil lead with her thumb.
I'm certain Francis Bacon
was a realist.
My self-portraits
resemble his
if you exclude talent
and that look of having razors
for skin. Rembrandt's hands
and mine could be twins
except mine are mute. I draw
my wife by touching her.
When she asks

what I'm looking for
under her skirt, I whisper
art.

Suggested modifications

I'd like my ears sewn over my eyes
so I can see what I'm listening to.
It will turn out that grass
is someone's sky, someone with face
buried in the earth and looking
up through clouds of dirt.
And why no Parade for Potato Salad,
third Saturday in July, no
Spoon Day or Pet Your Can Opener
Day so we can finally honor that
which keeps us alive above that
which wants us dead. If my crotch
was where my tongue is
and vice versa, pants
would have a window and hats
would be mandatory and long
and kissing would be fucking
and fucking would be kissing
and an erection with lipstick
resembles what famous dictator?
Think of it: in the dream
your fingers are appendages of wind.
You are an intimate of corn,
a tickler of constellations.
And when you wake and reach
to scratch, there will be a breeze
at the end of your hand,
a cyclone at your disposal.
What a revolution
picking your nose, dialing the phone.
Phones no longer have dials
yet kids
don't question the phrase.
Nor are they inclined
to wear their hearts on their sleeves

because we've taught them
that fashionable skin is steel.

Ringing the bell curve

I'm doing a study on ambition.
For science
I say to participants
as I take their money.
If they run after me
but don't catch up
I write down that they're slow.
Those that catch me
but are ticklish I've labeled
the "giggling poor."
You see why I gravitated
to the social sciences.
I have a pool and you don't.
I have nomenclature
at my disposal.
I have your address
and an index
of your contortions.

Cleaning house

When we first moved in we wondered
how the empty house had eaten
without our spoons.
Our canoe was happy on the ocean
of radiant wood, floors
we paddled all night
because we were young
and sometimes our voices
let loose didn't return
so we traveled the house
in search of our echoes.
Then we discovered the phrase,
that would look nice
in the living room. We bought
a bookcase. When it appeared
down in the mouth, we bought
a chair to keep the bookcase
company and a rug to look up
to the chair and a subscription
to *Better Homes and Gardens*
so all our stuff could read
of their betters and aspire.
Soon we lived on the porch
with the rain because our bed
was the only place for our china
to sleep. One night my wife
had a dream, she woke
transformed into an oracle
when she said, if we threw out
the empty boxes
we could throw out
the boxes that are full
of empty boxes. This is why
I'm first in line
to kiss her skull.

So it began that piles grew
at the sidewalk for trash
and recycling, the telescope
that's secretly just a hideout
for spiders who doubt
the existence of spiders
on other planets,
the schizophrenic shirt
both stripes and dots, a basket
in the shape of the vicarage
at Bathgate, a wicker home
away from home for flowers
even though we keep ours
in the earth which is almost
everywhere under foot and certainly
born to the task. Hardest
were the journals and reviews
the library wouldn't take, your poems
and my poems, her poems and his,
the guy who just won the thing
you should have won and I
was trying to win
by strenuous visualization,
each day picturing a Niagara
of dollars crashing
into my account and throngs
pressing my similes
to their lips in a ritual
not unlike throngs
pressing my deep images
to their lips. It came down
to us or them, twelve years
stacked under stairs, beds,
a kitchen table made solely
of narrative verse,
a home-entertainment center
built of lyrics
to the beloved thigh

and cunning moon and the rose
of immaculate petals
and the rose
of intractable thorns. Sadder
yet was the garbage man
in pony tail and Marley t-shirt,
who hopped when he saw spines
neatly reposed in boxes,
who eagerly grabbed and flipped
one and another over
until he saw what was inside,
four in a row he whipped
into the gut of the beast
before he realized
this was the mother lode
of verse and then
just heaved the boxes whole
to their death. When he pulled
the lever that tells
the hydraulic cylinder
to move the piston that crushes
matter to a finer point,
you and I attained
a level of compression
unmatched in contemporary letters,
language so dense
that not even light can escape.
And I felt the presence
of our lips—how we dream of love,
how we say goodbye to a river—
in the scream of the machine
as it ate our words, a music
like everything the sea
has learned being spoken at once.

The ethics of self-serve

Between his car door and the door
of the gas station he chewed
his bottom lip off. It seemed
anyway to be gone though secretly
it was hiding in his mouth. This walk
took a year while the walk
from the creamy goodness
of the Hostess stand to where I lived
behind the register
took merely an hour in memory
though in truth maybe just
fifty five minutes passed.
During this eternity I watched him
with the comfort of invisibility, being
what metaphysicians would call
perceptually displaced
and physicians would call sober
to his fucked up. It was ludes
I could tell because each step
seemed an argument between two
kinds of rubber or a dance
between the fork-lift
of his left leg and the hyena
of his right, I knew
we were related to Silly Putty but not
how proximate in descent
or why reversion
to a protoplasmic state
was considered the hot time
otherwise known as Saturday night.
When the slow ship
of his brain finally moored he began
feeding the counter every trinket
the out-of-body experience
called his right hand

found in his pocket, lighter
and lint and money
in a sequence of bills he found
texturally familiar
though not denominationally
significant. At which point
I, eighteen and in need of a raise,
utilized the phrase *keep going*
until exactly way after
he'd given me far too much,
then walked him to the door
of an orange Datsun B-210.
I found there a driver
participating fully
in this cauliflower consciousness,
who seemed to be in no places
at once and still
I let them drive off
when a simple request
like can I borrow your knees
would have locked them
in the grip of rumination safe
as cement. It took years
to consider the red lights
and sirens that may have attended
their fun down the road
or the mother who picked up
a phone that night
only to drop a phone
that night and scream
into the carpet the noise
of all the gears of her blood
being stripped. As I remember
I said thank you, good night,
come again and walked a straight line
back to my post and felt clever
having robbed a man

with no mind and because
the root beer I was drinking
came free.

A Late Book Left Open

Nothing was obvious and it was this
They began to celebrate after the rain
Who had first seen this had seen wonder
And returned to his wife and good sons
Happy with [the mystery / the history]
In the barley field the camel that he saw
On the far hill was a stone a mere stone
And on it he had carved once an angel

And there it was still the wing the garment
The glance the smudge where the kiss [a sneer /
A parabola] was hard as the stone [the shared
Edge / prayer dregs / *amen*] *Nothing*
Was obvious and his wife pelted him
[Obscure] not this *I love you but* shit shouted
As he danced the room the good dog barked
This is a late book [the wisdom / the problem]

Is open to interpretations
Note the angel never spoke [refers
To the promises / the premises of God]
And when he did return to his same wife
He filled his arms with her [Here the blessing /
No here] *Nothing was odious* nothing
Not the dog with the breath of lamb
Not the wife adrift in her loneliness

Not the fire that laughed when it died
And as he danced his legs out over
The far hill and back he stumbled and fell
In the rain [the stone / the readiness]
And the angel glanced yes nostalgic
For the not-obliterated presence what
Was not an absence also and so recognized
Possibly the loneliness the dance interpreted

The One Playlet for Public Consumption

The one good light
through which they pass
Outranks the servant and her ideal donkey
Breathing martyred hee-haws
And trying as best they can to carry the world

Very funny no enemy eh
God did you forget
[*Silence*] [*Disgusted pacing*]

When you said meet here
by the spruce tree and here it is
First spruce best spruce
[*Louder*] A spruce I could believe [*Louder*]
And yonder beyond it beyond a living doubt

Your helicopter growls
[*Growls*] and nowadays
To have a helicopter

This huge and tooled to drop
[*The donkey drops*]
Or orchestrate the drop of bits of food
And chocolate on the audience
Is plain and plump a miracle a motor miracle

Proving good intentions
To more susceptible souls
Proving liberty

Like a forest bird a whirring
liberty authentically loud
For in the beginning size noise [*Rapture*]
A thunderous clattering chocolate
No harm in chocolate

And first do no harm
If liberty is harmless
You understand the act

Liberating mainly those who help us
open up our interests
Sounds harmless enough to me
And of [*Oomph*] inherently national interest
[*Pleased*] It is to me [*Points*] as writ in simple sentences on leaflets

In nine or even fifteen
Enduring dialects
I told you people never read

Whereupon you said they may
[*Clapping hands*] They might
Goin down the hope slope
Are ye missy yawp nope
Hopalong hope

The earliest use of hope
In public [*Horrified*]
Was more or less a ropeadope pawn to potency

"In silence and in hope [*Salute*]
shall be our strength"
Eureka [*Begrudgingly*] Urethra
[*They droop swan-like to the wing and croon
Part frog part flutter passing on a fart sonata*]

Very funny first aid
Bloody colloquial music
For hypothetical hoi polloi

Sing O little tongues
for the courage of comedy
In a war stampede
The boring war the far far more sore war
Than any chore you knew before

Poor war your war snore
Gwan an beat their swords to pleasures
Their politics to soporifics

Their neverlasting pleasures perspicacity
[*Nodding feeling wise*]

Hush for now she enters finally in lion fur hurrah
Physically imposing military precise
[*And to no one in particular but light*]

FEW LINES WERE GIVEN TO ME
AND NONE OF THEM REVENGE
NONE ROMANTIC ANGST

YET NOW YE MARTYRS
SCATTER YE MORTARS
COME WHAT MAY [*They bow*] [*They taste her gown*]
"Necessity permits the forbidden"
[*Licking thinking*] handing down

The one last syllable
Of civility
To hyperbole

[*Offended*] Call it prayer
God did you forget
"Necessity" [*She leaves*]
Forgot the enemy [*Silence*] a little belated enemy
[*Silence again*] Suffering succotash [*They look aghast*]

Any soul reduced
To succotash suffers
Ask a lima bean

[*To the audience*] Who here dares
cast the first bean
Hugging the field in shriveled green moonlight
A show of hands [*Pause*] [*Shock*]
I told you people every one of them will cast another away

Is it over yet [*Pause*]
[*A dark cloud a clattering*]
Where's my bliss among the difficulties

[*Pause*] [*A cloud of chocolate*]
[*A cloud of succotash*]
Where's anything [*A roar and then a chorus*]
Beyond a cry of pain
That could be mine it could

Well did you ever ask it
Cry of pain will you be mine
Give it a pet a pat

Ashes to ashes begin the begat
or simply put it down in a basket
[*Singing*] I have been the cry the pet and now the basket
The basket protecting genitals [*Ooo*] until its usefulness
My friend my usefulness

Our usefulness has ended
A kind of liberty
[*Thunder*] Very funny

A Merry River Being Better Than a Weary Meadow

For Elegy

Hear the boys that bless themselves

Ask the ones
                    Beating off
Ask for it
Now he passes

Now his boat
                    Fills with paperwhites
Pollen scribble
Winter boys the moon

The hard-won intimates herded off

Now he passes
                    As he ripens them
Hordes them
Coming out the crown the sun

The buttock's
                    Gull silhouette
Now he passes
Heaven passes on

Hear it follow him a ways

Psalm

For the flutes

Trust the flutes in their lament between a woman and a man
Whatever they say sounds like laughing
Reveling in heavenly dilemmas
In harmony in mint in phallic moonlight a cunt sun
Whatever the others say wandering away never believe it

For once you fall to your knees your brain in his mouth
Her kisses monotonous whether animals commandments
Whatever way you turn sounds like arguing
The jawbone of an ass in all sincerity
Trust the flutes in their lament between a woman and a man

Time

John Wayne cocking his hip
In Marlene Dietrich's dressing room.
You're a big palooka, she says
Eyeing him up and down, lighting
A cigarette. M'am, he says,
Then hesitates, growing leery ...
She hikes her dress to reveal
A watch strapped to an upper thigh.
We have time, she says

' ' '

A spiral on the tree trunk
Resembled an Asian woman
Dancing—and why not?
I'd sat on the same stump
For 3 and a half hours

    Dead trout on the beach
Salted with sand

Or staring at the dark hair on her arm
In the barn, the mounting
Nervousness of the horses

' ' '

You get to a point
Where you slide sideways
Like a truck on wet clay—

Afterwards, tilted in
This natural ditch
In woods, it's like you

Knew it was going to happen
Only you wouldn't admit it

Some of these situations
End up much worse than others,
He said

' ' '

Flipping through an argument
Days later, that subtle pressure
For equilibrium

Water filling the claw-foot tub
Outside. At noon
Leaning in the cabin doorway
While grosbeaks wander the ground
For what's alive and coming
To the surface.

Eyes

A block from where the auditorium
Used to be, newspapers and damp stucco

Riddled panels, a seeping cold
Out of passages from another century

People in doorways looking for deals

One remembers
Snow like this from black & white movies,
Dropping straight down in front of windows,
Farther out
It shoots at a healthy slant

Someone bending to poke
Through the trash bin (where I threw chicken bones
the afternoon before). Over coffee, sitting in my overalls ...

On the street they hug their sleeves,
The sky descends to the level of eyes. Myself
At nineteen, attempting to grow a beard

A mirror held by Jesus
The fusty allure of old toys

Foxing books, mottled wallpaper

The policeman, priests,
The counter man at the liquor store locking
Or unlocking his door

Ha ha, she breathed, do you like me
In this wig. By the time I reached home
It was morning, my mother was dressing for church

Tracks

Sucking on cough drops
Hunched under hemlocks

Lynx tracks, martin tracks
Deer tracks, tracks of my own

Crossed tracks, moronic tracks
Bear tracks, under skin-flint

Clouds, oaks stretching
Dully—the mistake in such

Stillness, as in monuments
And train tracks, squirrel

Tracks, brittle with ice
Set in snow

One grows lean

Like the last guard
On the last atoll whistling

Through crusty teeth
Tracks of ships, tracks of planes

Tracks of bugs—
Under baleful sky

Tracks of thoughts
On a rusty chain

Clanking into depths
Of unescorted hearsay

Fainter tracks of mice and voles

Turning 50

There was the dog show on tv. Around the corner
Wind was wrestling wires, cedar in the back
Swaying like bulky assassins. Who can
You believe in? Where once there was a barn
Yards now separate like pieces of pie
On a surveyor's map (curling in the closet).
Mickey says, despite all the corncobs
Of insight and expectation, what do we have?
If I ignore him he won't prepare my taxes—
How no one warned us analogies weren't true,
He rambles on. The damn terriers always win
I say. Why are you so fitful, so susceptible?
And so on. Pushing my faults around
Like an apple. Rumps of snow by morning
The furnace pounding, the neighbor's barking
Terrier. She's the one with tattoos
Like bluegills, he says. Places you don't
Want to see. Ok, I agree. I'll agree
To anything that doesn't have to do with money.
Nature is rude, decided the Rationalists
But I was tired of confrontation. Waking
In the middle of the night, the sky calm
With stars, I drank two lemonades I was so thirsty
Listening to Fats Waller on the radio

The Gangsters

1.

Mostly they miss
The tension of a bigger city—

Talking of Vegas
To themselves. It's simple
To grow a tad eccentric.
Buying elaborate neon
For walls inside their homes—
They idle at tables
Like smoking cigarettes ...

In dark sedans,
With nephews talking deer hunting
The practice of baiting,
They'll wait until skunks
Are flicking through the garbage
For a gambler sleeping
With a smug arm over his alarm clock

2.

The street cleaner
Rounding round the elbow on Perch Street ...

Trouble is, suburbia is too full
Of thoughtfulness

When I looked up, said his neighbor,
The clouds had formed
A whole string of vaginas ...
The time Augie's wife paid a prostitute
To give him a blowsy on his birthday,
Unaware she was his girlfriend

He felt betrayed, cornered.

There's always someone richer
And thinner, replied his wife,
Bending over to lift a box of Christmas lights.

He sat counting the buttons on his shirt,
Listening to Coltrane

Anne eventually left him, and town,
With the man
Who owned the Sunoco Station.

Augie, said Heinie, it's not the cold war
Anymore.
In the yard, thin gruel of dirt from rain
Over paving stones to the shed

RON RASH

Something Rich and Strange

She follows the river's edge downstream, leaving behind her parents and younger brother who still eat their picnic lunch. It is Easter break from school. Her father has taken time off from his job and they have followed the Appalachian Mountains south, stopping first in Gatlinburg, then the Smokies, and finally this river. She finds a place above a falls where the water looks shallow and slow. The river is a boundary between South Carolina and Georgia, and she wants to wade into the middle and place one foot in Georgia and one in South Carolina so she can tell her friends back in Pennsylvania she has been in two states at the same time.

She kicks off her sandals and enters, the water so much colder than she imagined, and quickly deeper, up to her kneecaps, surging under the smooth surface. She shivers. Fifty yards downstream a granite cliff rises two hundred feet into the air to cast this section of river into shadow. She glances back to where her parents and brother sit on the blanket. It is warm there, the sun full upon them. She thinks about going back but is almost halfway now.

She takes a step and the water rises a littler higher on her knees. Four more steps she tells herself. Just four more and I'll turn back. She takes another step and the bottom is no longer there and she is being shoved downstream and she does not panic because she has passed the Red Cross courses and is a lifeguard at the country club. The water shallows and her face breaks the surface and she breathes deep. She tries to turn her body so she won't hit her head on a rock and as she thinks this for the first time she's afraid and she's suddenly back underwater and hears the rush of water against her ears. She tries to hold her breath but her knee smashes against a boulder and she gasps in pain and water pours into her mouth. Then for a few moments the water pools and slows. She rises coughing up water, gasping air, her feet dragging the bottom like an anchor trying to snag a hold on waterlogged wood or jut of rock and as the current quickens again she sees her family running along the shore and she knows they are shouting her name though she cannot hear them and as the current turns her she hears the falls and knows there is nothing that will keep her from it as the current quickens and quickens and another rock smashes against her knee but she hardly feels it as she snatches another breath before the river pulls her under and she feels the river fall and she falls with it as water whitens around her and she falls deep into the whiteness and as she rises her head scrapes against a rock ceiling even as the hydraulic holds her under the boulder and she tells herself don't breathe but the need rises inside her beginning in the upper stomach then up through her chest and throat and as that need reaches her mouth her mouth and nose open simultaneously and the lungs explode in pain and then the pain is gone as bright colors shatter around her like glass shards, and she remembers her sixth grade science class, the gurgle of the aquarium at the back of the room, the smell of chalk dust that morning Mr. Marston held a prism out the window so it might fill with color, and she has a final, beautiful thought—that she is now inside that prism and knows something even Mr. Marston does not know, that the prism's colors are voices, voices that swirl around her head like a crown, and at that moment her arms and legs she did not even know were flailing cease and she becomes part of the river.

The three rescue squad members and the sheriff got to the falls late in the afternoon. Two of the rescuers were brothers, one in his early twenties, the other thirty. They had their own carpentry business, mainly building patios and decks for lawyers and doctors from Greenville and Columbia who had second homes here in the mountains. The third man, the actual diver, was in his early forties and taught biology at the county high school. The sheriff and the others had had to wait until he finished his last class before gathering here.

The sheriff looked at his watch and figured they had an hour and a half at most. Even so the diver did not hurry to transform himself into something black-skinned and amphibious. He smoked a cigarette and between puffs told a joke he'd heard from one of his students. Only the brothers seemed impatient. The sheriff and diver had worked together before. They knew death, unlike life, did not require haste.

When the diver was ready a long length of nylon rope was wrapped and clasped tight under his arms. The older, stronger of the brothers held the rope's other end. As the diver waded into the river the rope trailed behind him like what it was—a leash.

When the water rose to his chest he dipped his mask in the water, put it on, and leaned forward. The water was clear, and the three men on the shore watched as the black fins propelled the diver away from them and into the hydraulics' unending blizzard of water.

When he'd disappeared completely the men on the bank sat on rocks and waited. The older brother with the rope in his hand pointed upstream where the river bent right. He told how he'd caught a five-pound Rainbow Trout there last fall. The sheriff asked what he'd used for bait, but didn't hear the answer because at that moment the sheriff saw a mask bobbing in the whitewater below the hydraulic.

The brother with the rope tightened the slack and pulled but nothing gave until the others grabbed the rope as well. They pulled the diver into the shallows with the rope and then with their hands dragged him onto shore where he lay coughing up water and gasping air.

It took him a few minutes before he spoke. He told them how he had found her in the undercut behind the hydraulic. She had been upright, her head and back, and arms and legs pressed against a flat rock slab. Only her hair moved, long blonde hair that reached toward the surface like tendrils. Her blue eyes had been open, the diver said, watching as he came closer so he might embrace her. He had been trying to wrap his arms around her waist when it happened. His eyes and hers were mere inches apart, and something had happened the moment before the hydraulic had ripped free the mask and mouthpiece.

He told the men who kneeled beside him that her blue eyes had had life in them. He told how he could feel the beating of her heart against his chest and that as his head pressed close to hers she had whispered something to him. He told the other men he would never enter the river again.

The younger brother scoffed out loud, while the older spoke of narcosis of the deep though the pool below the falls was no more than twenty feet at the very most. But the sheriff did not dismiss what the diver said. He too had seen things involving the dead that had he spoken of them would have been as strange and inexplicable as the diver's words. But he had never mentioned such things to others and did not choose to now. We'll have to find another way, he told the men on the shore. That river's going to have to drop some before I allow another diver in there.

He had trouble going to sleep that night. Every time he closed his eyes he saw the wide blue eyes, the yellow hair flowing upward. His wife slept beside him, her back curled into his chest and upper knees. They had no children, had wanted none, and now he was more than ever glad this was so. He had seen a picture of the parents in the local weekly paper. They had been on the shore, within thirty feet of the undercut that held their daughter, the expressions on the parents' faces beyond grief, something hard and implacable and expressionless—like river rock worn smooth by torrents of water.

When he finally did sleep the girl came with him. They were in the river again and though he had no wet suit on the river was warm as bath water, water he could breathe in. There was no rope this time either, and as he embraced her she whispered to him that this world was better than the one above and she should never have been afraid to come here.

He emerged in the embrace of his wife, gasping for breath as she told him to calm down, that it was all a bad dream. She got up to use the bathroom and when she came back his back was turned to her and he appeared asleep. She closed her eyes and was quickly asleep again, but his eyes were not closed and after a while he went into the kitchen and graded lab tests until dawn.

The girl remained in the river. Volunteers cast grappling hooks from the banks and worked them like lures through the pool or stood in shallows or on rocks and jabbed with long metal poles, but the river gave up nothing. Some of the old-timers suggested dynamite but the sheriff and the girl's parents were both against that. The sheriff said what they needed was a week without rain.

The diver slept little the next few nights. In class he taught little. He placed the students in small groups and had them discuss assigned chapters among themselves. He knew they were not talking about pupae and chrysalides but talking instead of the prom and summer plans and he did not care. On the third afternoon after the last class left, he skipped a teacher's meeting and sat alone in his classroom. The school was quiet, quiet as only a school can be with its rippling wake of silence after the students have left. The only sound was the murmur of the aquarium by the window.

He would never speak to anyone, not even his wife, about what happened next. He could not even be sure he had closed his eyes. All he knew was he lay in the river and a gathering brightness surrounded him. He felt bits of himself break and glow and pulse like hearth-sparks and each bit of himself somehow carried all of what it had broken free of with it and he felt not only himself but the river expanding and he saw that what he was now was more than all the stars he had ever viewed through a telescope for they were within him now, and he understood what the girl had whispered to him, what she had wanted from him.

And then the sound of the janitor rolling his mop bucket down the hall, the gurgle of the aquarium. He called the sheriff that night and told him he'd dive for the girl again.

Days passed. Rain came often, long rains that made every fold of slant-land a tributary and merged earth and water into a deep orange-yellow rush more fire than water in its pure annihilation of what had been only hours before as it transformed sandbars and stick jams. Pools and eddies swelled and swiftened. Banks disappeared as though the river had reached out of itself and dragged them under.

But that was only surface. In the undercut all remained quiet and still, the girl's transformation unrushed, gentle. Crayfish and stone fly larvae unknitted flesh from bone, minnows and nymphs attentive to the loosed threads.

Then the rains stopped and the river ran clear again. Boulders that had vanished for weeks reappeared midstream. Sandbars and stick jams regathered in new places and configurations. The water warmed and caddis flies broke through the river's skin to make their ephemeral flights before falling back to their element.

The sheriff called the diver and told him the river was low enough to try again. The next day they walked the half-mile down the path to the falls. There were five of them this time, the sheriff, his deputy, the two brothers and the diver. The sheriff insisted on two ropes and he made sure the ropes stayed taut.

The water was clearer than last time, and the river offered less resistance as he swam into the whitewater. He entered the abeyance as though parting a curtain and entering a room. The river suddenly was muted, distant, his life to this moment distant too, all memory. It seemed he wasn't even in water.

She was less of what she had once been, the blue rubbed from her eyes, flesh freed from the chandelier of bone. He reached out and touched the bones of what had once been a hand. The river whispered to him that it would not be long now.

When he got back to shore he told them her body was gone, that not even a scrap of clothing or bone was there. He told them it had all probably been swept downstream by the last hard rain. The younger brother said the diver should go back in and search the left and right side of the falls. He argued the body could still be down there, its position shifted a few yards. The deputy suggested they lower an underwater camera into the pool.

The sheriff shook his head and said the diver was right, the body was the river's now. The men packed up their equipment and walked up the trail, back toward their vehicles, their lives. The mid-day sun leaned close and dazzling. Dogwoods bloomed and the woods they walked through seemed lit by small white stars. The diver knew in another week the petals would begin to fall from the branches and white patches would appear in the wood's under story, but some of the petals would fall in the river. They would gild the backs of pools and midstream rocks and snags. They would drift onto sandbars and settle in the silty beds of pools. The diver knew some would drift through the rapids and over the falls into the hydraulic. They would form a swirling constellation and then and only then would the bones break free from one another and the constellation would expand and keep on expanding until it contained a whole river.

Daedalian

...your cobbled wings
then struck me: blue,
soon to be as absent as sky.
What could I have said midflight?
                                        "The keel in your breast, boy!"   ?
A blue cage in my mouth,
shameful sediment of desire.
How you spiraled and arced,
the smoking wax in my throat.
After the plunge of your body,
                                        a single feather
                              then another
      and another
papered the vast sea.
(Where was the crone that morning
with her uninvited forecast?
I'm tired of hearing about what we did do)

:your foolishness, my foolishness.

I am now prepared
to feel my way down the dark sides
of the riddles unto death.
O do be wordless.
Something sweet and red
fertilizes regret:
sugar rotting the apple.
The thrum of our hearts, or
Beat...   Beat...
The worked muscle of strong wingbones.
A series of fortunes. A long story
always eventually stopped short.
                                        And still, we flew

My Dearest Memory

In this dream I must selectively
apply the law of gravity to myself
or I fly off the world.

My father is taking place
on a boat watching the sunset.
He wears his reading glasses.

Not a dream, a memory: this is

the real day I am flying
off the dock because
One Must Learn To Swim

Sometime.

As I am falling,

my father occurs to me
as the best audience
the sky has ever had:

He never interrupts.

Wait. Did my father wear glasses?
It must not be him in the boat.

Plunged cold
in my lungs
the whole sky is lost
someone always saves me
hilarious to breathe
once saved

Memory
of a memory
I do remember
remembering it
vividly

Oh yes,

My father happens
to have always worn glasses.
It is him. Or else he is
wearing his glasses someplace else.

Another real time.

If that is him
out in the middle of the lake,
who pushes me in? And who
eventually fishes me out?

Birds of Appetite

Sometimes I'm sure my body still lies
across every patch of land it's ever lain.

More forgotten than the naked Barbie dolls
on every shelf of every second-hand store

across This Great Country.
And don't wings sprout

from the things which root in me.
They pulse and pull outward

a green thumb which bores me to tears
which water things. Ho-hum.

The jungle of yard goes to pot.
Am I not what you'd call a pack-rat?

I'm late for the gym
where I like the treadmill.

I think everybody likes the treadmill,
but the garbage man

is blocking my way with his truck.
All the things that didn't go in the rummage sale:

a collection of state spoons with no Alaska,
a Graceland T-shirt, a cage with no bird.

When was there ever a bird?
Most things appear

from out of nowhere, and I'm told it can't be helped.
As they say, You Can't Happen

In The Same Shit Twice. As I say,
a more logical explanation would be grand.

Should life around here get a little rougher for the crows?
One day it really might.

To A Margin

for/after Sarah Fox

Dear S,
The shape of time is not stone
today, it is forward.
Not less than arrows
or the speed of height.
No more stone than
what equals sand
-(-x)thousands.
Today the shape of time
is softer than death plus one.
Stop-winged but infinitely sky.
Adding positives to negatives
at a chalkboard until
you want to pass out
in front of the upper classmen.

Dear S,
The shape of time leaves
shadows we call "I made this"
we call "memories" we call
"smoking." There shift scenes,
a bad actor's shadow over
all the lines greased down
a squeaky face who reads
"but I feel nineteeeeeen."
Kill mirrors.

Dear S,
Today the shape of time
is mimicking your shape thinking
Babies? I could have babies....

Dear S,
Solution is the way
our play bodies take everything in,
make anything, including terrible stops
and detailed paintings of lives. Still. We dissolve.
Time and salt have the whitest wedding.
I think I'll cry real tears
every second it happens.

Dear S,
Yes.
Time with its stone shape
did then *renounce it all to a margin.*

Dear S,
The push of a tree
throwing leaves at you: Fall-time.
I know orange like a stone's seed.
Like an orange.
Time lurks/ time couldn't
care less about lurking.
It's so omnipresent
it forgets itself before we do.
Tying our shoes for work
we did bore/are boring/
will bore time to death.

Dear S,
You know every little pebble
in a highway (la la la?) Time
could only want knees
to skin on each.

Success

Success as the result of industry is a peasant ideal.
– Wallace Stevens

When the motors we've heard turn over for as long as childhood
hang clouds of exhaust dead or alive on driveways,
and the lawyer neighbor always steps inside his car, quiet as a
funeral,

and his wife walks to her private college library job,
a Walkman balanced in one palm like Augustine's City of God,
a cathedral buttressed by lasers so the songs and talk shows

can cross the glib green daybreak—dawn of spittle,
this surface-health is mostly surface wealth.
These neighborly squares of Chemlawn grass

are cobwebbed with these forms that first shoot through
a few square millimeters of arachnid neural cord
from some first distant reach success perfected,

all the way from the dawn of connection.
Trapdoor spiders leave to us their successful vortices.
Success has no head or time for sullenness or anger—

from the very dawn of want it spools our walks
between the house and the little liquor store.
Its late-Rothko window—neon's success at a signature.

And sometimes, often, no one in the aisles,
except for the clerk who may also have his habits—
see him, holding my twenty to the light

now, here, abundantly, exactly the way
people die on the strength of what they've done to each other.

' ' '

But its dawn and the doors push back the light
before the light successfully comes in—
Then the light was never there, shame on it.

The night comes in and walks right through our rec rooms.
In fog our houselights seem as jacklit fauna.
Houses brighten or darken, as faces darken

Or brighten, one at a time, one at a time—
the way people die, or look up at the sky.
Success is like that and it is not like that.

That which happened in the sequel, termination of all affairs,
first wing brush and the subsequent spasms,
success without pause spooling out our days

past skateboards lying on their aching backs—

' ' '

What is fortune but outward accident
for a few years sixty at most and gone,
said Blake, obliged to illustrate egg cups, tureens, crockeries, call-
ing cards—

Fame if you win it lasts just a minute croons
Tony Bennett in "Make Someone Happy"—
and sometimes I do, you do, we smile past knowledge—

the neighbor's dog stops squealing like a saxophone
and I can stop trying not to pray for its death. *Mercy*
is to praise—to be forgiven for fame alone—said Coleridge.

Mercy me (James Brown) to understand whether it was fame
or something less addressable, some life buried out loud,
while it was breathing, Coleridge asked forgiveness for.

They say he learned how to talk even when he was asleep.
I've paged through lifetimes, through necrologies
with no words coming out of them that do not talk

of even better words: the words that got us here
may get us out of here but not our poorest failures—
long after success is finished looking out of us

success may have walked through the fire of success
and somehow not have been consumed
so that what is formed of the ashes can rise up to slay us.

' ' '

Our neighbors and us, we're forced to talk sometimes
if it snows too hard, we're happy to, we unbury our cars
and even if the rest of the year we look away

it's partly in dejection we look away.
And "the purely reflective merely partakes of death. . . ."
The nearly undetectable derision of good friends,

rubbing each other the wrong way, disingenuous praise—
I feel more gone from the close friends than the far ones—
each trying to finish a book, a life, a family,

each success muttering to clothe me, feed and fuck me,
each having to be pulled back from any boat
he made, if only to be made to enter that boat.

2

in the name of this organic and original naturalness
of the body we declare and wage war on drugs
– Derrida

What a life is the eye, Coleridge said.
It's good to romance the Romantics, a well meaning
mistaken friend said (may she find true romance,

each instant boundless with necrologies. . .)
Or another friend who stole a numbered gravestone
and cleaned its beveled integers with a toothbrush—

her shrink said she was *taking care of herself.*
As for the widest friendship, it is a tiny town.
As for the world of *resist*, as for where we live now,

as for all these friends, only some of them forgot
us first, only some were put down in the books
in black and white, as we say when we want it in writing

because *God's rainbow will* is nothing I can read.
Because nature is another dawn unworldly and orange.
Because we hand ourselves perpetually

over to a night to which we are party—
Wasn't he a drug-addict? Another friend,
He was I hear myself say. . . .

Cigarette smoke it'd take and axe to cut,
speaking animals tipping beers—
The Green Top Lounge where we shall drink to our friends . . .

to be taken care of by nothing we can betray—
to friendship *addicted*—which once meant "devoted, bound,
delivered over to"—
harsh success looks out at harsh success.

Across the street some kids pile out of a bus
to play rock-n-roll at a failed movie theatre.
These human amps for blackness in their black,

turn on the lights, faces of girls and boys say,
turn on the town, eyes open to bright night
and aren't the street lights just as addicted,

glacial-slow police cars looking for easy fish,
the sulfur flaring in puddles we walk across
to the open coffin of our car—

' ' '

Crack Wars. In an altogether uncanny manner, the polemics surrounding drugs historically became a War only when crack emerged. Crack lost its specificity as merely one drug among others. As synecdoche of all drugs, crack illuminates an internal dimension of polemos—opening the apocalyptic horizon of the politics of drugs.
– Avital Ronnell

Whatever we most fear, we mostly are.
Success this, success that. Coleridge took his life
for all that life was worth and still it was

a life like a zero of breath on a window.
It was like this small-town's crack-infested life—
a prostitute talking a mile a minute,

pulling out a pliers-bent antenna for a pipe.
O but the single instance scarcely existed—
too poor this one, for a glass pipe, her eye whites crazed with capillaries,

branching out like the shaken oaks, and pipeheads
walking as the memory of elms
past the cinder block Powerhouse Church of God,

the Polar Bear Liquors with its neon polar bear,
The Beehive Foods, the Company Store—
just one hit—outside already inside—

occupied, everybody on the dotted line—
nullified to synecdoche, for now
the bar lights had spread filaments everywhere

and the night swung its censor of car exhaust,
streetlights stretching out an ellipsis. . . .
Crack, sheer success, the fast-food drug without

a speaker shaped like a clown to shout your order in,
cheese crumb for a mousetrap, the size of the "tiny"
you find in "infinity,"

a little revelation, something to put in the pipe.
Sometimes someone gets in and you go for a ride somewhere.
She took a hit, I breathed her spirit in me—

inhaled, and my life held her breath as I breathed in,
as the lights of night sparkling with lives inside
are all the dots there are for such as us to connect—

3

And it all comes back now: warzone: hapless success:
groups of dealers still and rustling as trees.
Once around the Northside to check for dragnets,

up Church, left on Patterson,
right on Cobb to North, right on North
to a left onto Park—nautilus-like involvulus

and orthogonic spiral—
to Westnedge, street named after a slaughtered colonel.
I'm driving down the avenue of vanishing—

that any pitiable individual instance
can scarcely exist at all,
an almost nonexistent fingernail-

dip into the tiny bat—what kind of shit am I—white shit—
immediately abstracted—peasanted—
occupied, every body on the dotted line—

no voice but this could come so close
to life without living into another—
everyone pulled their own face off—

the Pizza-Hut neon was still on from the night before,
snowmelt shining on wet asphalt, more
falling from nowhere we can see, therefore

like some dedication utterly without beginning.
Pigeons eyelashing the Burger King sign.
Pigeons, unlike humankind, bear everything.

There I am, just like a human being:
Humankind is not a very outgoing thought.
There, my profile—is it a signed confession?

She ripped me off, isn't that the American
way? She broke off a piece from my chip
(me, what serious druggies called merely a chipper)

and set it next to her brother watching television.
It was a quiet offering, a charity,
it was as unsolicited as love,

it was my chip and it was smaller now.
Can we do better with our compassions or our prisons?
Drug dough cooked up in cookie pans,

it's a sad thing when you look at it
but whoever did and now the law's involved,
now I can be arrested like an image,

immediately abstracted by pure need,
and suddenly feel a coroner's skin
draw tight upon my own,

—inside that place where no light shines
what thou has entered here is thine
own now, no one else can get inside here. . . .

(1992-94)

4

New stupefactions reel out of the dawn,
something in me looks up when the cat looks up and I still don't
    hear—
Mostly survival is just not properly wired to hear.

That's success breathing life into all the passing faces,
success forgets the best idea of survival toward care it sometimes is,
new dawns eat away all other dawn,

and through each dawn is such good sight of our neighbors,
what we see is both there and not there,
just as our most substantial honesties are shadows,

are human and the cars don't sound like the ocean,
they don't unroll their sounds like Grecian scrolls,
they sound like tired voices stepped back off the docks again—

. . .

The spiders wait out flies in their guy-wired clouds of spit,
brocading the trapdoor webs also with moths
like dusty rooftops, and breakable deep grubs.
With day my neighbor drives off, his wife walks all the way
to her job of filing the good blindnesses of books,
their children drive to college and come back

like human boomerangs and are looking successful—
success is habit, and habit a policeable thoroughfare,
cop cars knifing each noon down our street.

For days and days I felt a coroner's skin
drawn tight upon my own. Now I shall be a lamb.
But not John Lamb, murdered murderer, Tex #587,

dead by the hand of the scabrous body politic—Nov. 10, 1999,
"It was almost as if I was shooting my bad luck or something."

' ' '

I want a lullaby like a little bag.
I want a success I can breathe.
I want to star in a silent movie about silence

that like all silence has no vocabulary to speak of.
I want to put down all my murdering wants
and feed them dog food for the rest of their hell.

While the webs and the chain-link fences are where the daylight
is shining in dew-drop bedecked barbed accordion wire
around the Mercedes dealership and the fasttalk salesmen,

hood ornaments, beautiful, untouchable, beyond my want,
light fortunate beyond all lullaby,
awake forever after in this past

which sometimes prays, but it's only blood that kneels,
every drop we've shed, or better, haven't, not
this time, this time, my little lies like lambs—

dawn again is the bread that crumbles softly
till another night shall reveal its handful of cares,
the spiders sleep, the stars sink to the human.

I Think Words Louder

I think words louder when mother wants
help cooking and fingerspells slowly.
There is plenty of room for talking
after dinner on the couches, brother forgets the words
sometimes: coffee cup, tomato, business, lousy,
and I know he only tells me the good stuff.

Mother wants to know if we want dessert
and is only up to the "E" before I know.
Aunt Louise is talking loudly,
Margaret keeps smiling at me from across the table

and brother is telling a joke.
He's running, he's looking back
and the gorilla's huge and he picks her up
and tells her he wants to get married and smushes her in his
 hands:
I'm laughing because it's a deaf joke
because Alice is here,
because Alice never knocks and mother thinks it's rude
and I think Alice thinks she's knocking, and I can't stop laughing
because mother won't say it and she knows.
Mother is never sure if you sign fast enough.
She is up to the "P" when Alice says sure
and now brother is laughing and mother is sure of it.

Brother's drinking beer on the couch, slurring his signs,
making up conversations because mother would never say that.
I'm thinking my words out, about Aunt Louise's perfect teeth,
about father who taps on the table,
about Alice who must make noise when she chews.
Times like these I am backwards, like watching an eyelid or a
 mouth

opening and closing and my brother is standing there pointing
and I can't think of a name for it
and Alice squeezes my hand under the table
like she's got something to tell me.

Hadrianus

Stores disappear like streets when a day falls inside me
and I am standing by the covered couch in your living room,
and you are rolling socks into drawers, the glass case
by your bed with your phone number written inside it,
your pills crushed in half on the counter.
Pills that you tried not to take, that brought you sleep under covers
where you block out sunlight with pillows.
As I walk into the parking lot, I trip over the snow,
like one trips out of a dream; I keep falling over things that don't exist.
We are at the reservoir and you are excited by the black flies,
you must have forgotten to shave
and there's this rock in the road that I am thinking about kicking,
I'm thinking about kicking it all the way to the truck,
200 should do it, when you say, "Marry me,"
and I bargain with the trees for words.

Your blue sweater that I'm wearing makes me think of you
introducing yourself to philosophers, "Socrates, Hadrianus; Plato,
    Hadrianus,"
holding out your hand for them to take.
I can't help wanting to dance with you in the supermarket
and tell people we met when we crashed bicycles,
everything starts taking forever.

There was a bookstore at the end of the street.
The streets walk with us, and there's a picture of North Hampton,
it looks nothing like it, but I have to stop,
because the picture is changing the town and I like it better this way.

Sometimes I walk down a neighborhood where the pictures
are better than the town
the benches are perfect for sitting.
Once in a while a day drops out of me,
but most of the days I can't catch,
it's getting so terribly late so quickly.

Somebody Else's Funeral

Trees like bones waving outside this window.
Mexico's way of keeping graveyards above ground,
you ask me to promise never to let a black boxcar
take you to the parlor when you see one crossing the road.
This is somebody else's funeral.
A man perhaps who has lost his son to cancer.
Two years of doctors watching a boy fall into his bed.
He was young, and because of this, failed to keep any of his friends
who were mad to attend and their parents
who are thankful because of course this is not their child.
There will be no Kaddish, no open casket.
He will be taken to the graveyard that looks upon the apartments.
For now the crying is loud and the face still raw outside his yard,
the school emptied out for a day of prayer.
Maybe it was a woman, and a man she no longer knew
walked up behind her like she always knew would happen
and took her under the throat and she couldn't get the screaming out.
The man is here, this is what he does, he attends funerals.
Maybe she was screaming and people were watching from their car
windows
hoping the screaming would stop.

Right now the parents are in their television rooms
giving themselves up to a god they once believed in.
They are taking back conversations:
if only he hadn't let him go out that night,
if she had kept a better dressed daughter.

CHRISTINE SCHUTT

A Day, A Night, Another Day, Summer

On the first night they took her to the locals' favorite for lobster, she got sick, and they consoled her home with excuses. It must have been the boat to the island and the egg-white scum that spilled from the claws when she cracked them. It must have been the distance she had traveled to visit. Imagine their surprise! Suddenly, their daughter's girl, knocking open the screen door, carrying a string bag of oranges, a few clothes and some tapes, no plans, but an appetite, it seemed, for what the island fetched up in traps. Lobster, her favorite, although the face she wore on their walk back home was cast down and waxy. Ellen put her to bed while he looked at the sky and thought how sad a girl could be at twenty.

He was eighty; live long enough a phrase astutter in his brain. *Live long enough* to see the children's children shrivel into age. The world tilts. The light is a blunt knife that shucks a man awake; the sky is the milky blue of an oyster. No sun, in fact, yet an old man will feel it. He wakes and his freckled hands tremble. Yes, he would like to tell his granddaughter, this girl, his only, what it means, really, to be *eighty* and alive.

"That old!" she gasped when in the morning they spoke.

"Yes, I am, and I know things. Be happy. Don't wait."

He struck up the fire and stayed haunched to watch it take; in the kitchen Ellen frittered at their breakfast. Eat, drink. This was a treat for them, Ellen was saying; it was not every day their granddaughter visited, and they were happy to see her. Happy again, the word sprung wild as the island's regal wagging, fields of weedy purples and golds, red geraniums against the chalky houses. Their umpteenth summer here alone, his and Ellen's, and they woke to the weather, pleasure-bent.

Old folks' pleasure, maybe; maybe that was what the girl would call it. Seed-dry and slow—too many books, no TV; birds their only entertainment. Old folks they were with old folks' ways. The temperature's night-plummet meant it was cold when they awoke, and he often made a fire.

He had been laying kindling when the girl shuffled in, wearing a blanket—no robe—next morning.

"Charlotte," Ellen said—"aren't you cold?"

No, thank you, yes, thank you, no was his granddaughter speaking—the darling! Look at the bits of cloth she wore when she was dressed. No breasts. Jutted movement, bones—her bones, Charlotte's—were handles, too visible. She had what so many girls had that made them turn their bodies into spears. Wingblades and wrist bones, bones, bones, a girl sharply outlined; her eyes fixed on the water were a murk.

"I feel as if I haven't been here in such a long time," she said.

He reminded her of what she needed to know if she should go out in the boat. The cove. The lily pond. The ledge where the eagles nested.

They kept the house door unlocked—"Remember?"

"Crime is everywhere, Poppie. Even here," she said, but he laughed.

He said, "You don't need to drive anywhere, but I trust you with the car." He said this although he wasn't sure. Never had he seen the girl off but he thought she would fail. This girl, he thought, was so much like his daughter, and he watched as she swayed down the path swopping branches. Was she talking to herself?

II

Charlotte said her mother always expected to see a prettier daughter. This was on the porch, when they sat, the three of them, in the low, wet light of the morning and watched the waves in their halfhearted slash against the shore. Charlotte sighed in the lugubrious haul to noon, the trudging drudgery of remembering those other gardens where Charlotte said her mother wandered overdressed and spectral. He could see this figure, yes, and the murmurous plaint of Charlotte's voice reminded him of his daughter's voice. "Mother says she is a very good camper," and Charlotte made a little sound, a little laugh, but then, it seemed, she saw what he saw and, made afraid, turned quiet.

III

He thought umpteen years when he calculated time on the island with only his wife, but in total, as a family, it was fifty years—hardly umpteen—summer after summer in the cranky rusticator, brambled, slanted, salt-bleached. Dishes of opened mussel shells blued the bathroom vanities, stones from the beach held back books. Faded top sheets in faded seaglass colors—green, blue, yellow, pink—poufed in the wind unanchored by the blankets Ellen kept in chests. After breakfast every morning Ellen opened the bedroom windows wide to the sea and let the air light and lighten the house even as he nudged the fire downstairs. Years with and without a daughter: the fire, the airing.

"Your grandmother and I are here to be happy," he said when Ellen was gone with her basket and shears. He said, "Try to be happy yourself while you're here," and he walked off the porch towards the water. If his knees could be oiled, he thought, he might reach the shore faster.

IV

"This is serious," Charlotte said, and she lolled on the dock with him and talked about school and her father and Tibet and the environment and her father (again) and the criminal amounts of money made on Wall Street. "I mean I'm glad for Daddy and all, but there are too many poor people in the country."

"Swim!" he said. "The water is not so cold."

V

Lunch, and he told the girl to eat her pickle before he did. What he loved about the girl were the girlish parts. How she broke up a muffin to find the berries and pelleted the cakey crumbs to feed the chickadees; the way she called to all living things in a small voice, purely, he loved this much about her, and the way she licked her lips or twisted her hair when she was thinking. Her far-off face when she was thinking, her flush, her breaths. The shallow pan of breastbone, her close, small ear. Darling girl, his darling, he confused her sometimes with his daughter.

Ellen was saying, "They have said they will call us when they think we can visit her."

He wished his granddaughter had gone somewhere else to rest. He wanted no more stories about his daughter. He was too old. Old, sick, set back by the same news that his daughter was not happy. "I was tired last night, Poppie, if that's what you mean. I don't get sick often."

He asked, "So why don't you eat instead of picking?" How he must look to her—beaked, lidded, wattled, a moody old man with shames and losses, very few friends, no hobbies. Crabbed, sullen, closed off, somehow failed. All he had done was make money, money, money enough to buy a summer house when he was yet young and then old, old for a long time and time long enough for his daughter to squander lots of it—money.

He said, "You'd do well to think of what's happened to her." He was about to say more when Charlotte began to cry.

VI

How he had found his bedroom, he could not remember; but the sun through the trees turned the surface of his bed to water; the light was astir on his bed, and he knew, at least, that it was late afternoon, the bay calmed, the water too blue and sun-scratched to look at. He knew he had slept and that the shrill part of the day was over; the house was very quiet. Stillness, the quiet of the wholly present-tense, the luxurious absence of melancholy, ire and whatever other meanness switched him through the house, all was easy and now. Now and now and now. He stepped onto the porch with a dish of peanuts and his drink, his glasses, his book. Heart's-ease at dusk, the sky orange-edged at first, then smoked. "Ellen!" he was calling. "You're missing this. Come look!" but she was already just behind him, humming approvingly at the plummy sworl of clouds.

But here they come, the two of them, in a hospital room, blood-

ed with sunset, his daughter and his granddaughter. His granddaughter saying, "It's the flu, Poppie. There's no reason to be sad. Mommy's coming home soon."

"Jimmy," Ellen said, "Charlotte is asking you a question," and she was shaking him back to the porch and the girl who was grown. The glass in his hands was empty; peanut casings, salt, a ring of wet from the sweated drink were all that was left of the sunset.

His daughter is combing with her fingers what is left of her hair. Her face is flat against a screen. She is talking but he doesn't know about what.

See the candles, the watery surface of the cake aflame—whose?

Balloons, brushed against, snap, and her fine hair stands on end, and her black patent leather shoes make staticky cracks, and a little girl cries, "They bite!"

The febrile sensation of sunburn that had put him to sleep woke him to the religious blue and evening damp near dinner and Ellen asking, "Are you cold, dear?" saying, "Charlotte, darling, get Poppie his jacket, will you?"

"I'm not hungry," he said. "I feel sick."

VII

Ellen brought him beef broth and would gladly have sat on the next bed watching if he hadn't said go on, go on, go on, and when Ellen asked again, "Are you sure . . ." he frowned at her until the door shut softly, and she was gone.

He slept. His dreams closed sharply as chapters, and he woke every time to spooky no-man's hours and the sensation of distant sleepers until he saw the shape he knew for his wife: a fizz of gray, a forehead, brown mouth. The room cohered. The table, the dresser, the lamp, the rug seemed no longer some dead man's effects, but his again, familiarly attached, and he stood, whole and unencumbered, watching the glaucous outdoor colors deepen. A windless hour, the spruce still, and he could hear, or thought he could hear, the gurgle of low-tide, its stinky, hissing bounty.

He had had a daughter once. She picked the shore to fill glass globes with decorative reminders of the sea. Ever a brooder, weeping over the irretrievable summer, she let the anger rise in her, like a tide, until it brimmed and spilled and ended in small violence, smashing the glass globes against the bathroom tiles and walking through the house in bloody feet.

The morning yellowed and the tide, he saw, coming in, but the wet slats of the dock were yet damp or he would sit; instead, he picked his way to the granite shelf that was a distance from the dock and long enough in light to have visibly dried, dulled, turned pink; and here he sat, for a long time sat, proudly agile, an old, old man—eighty!—in only a flannel robe, thin pajamas and boiled wool slippers, all gifts his wife insisted on. *Wear them, Jimmy or you'll catch your death!*

"Poppie!"

Charlotte, he saw, all elbows and knees, was zigzagging, towards him, happy. "Poppie! What are you doing out here in your robe? Gra-mum says to come in and get warm."

VIII

"Ellen, Ellen, Ellen, for God's sake, please!" He was looking in the bird book for what had flown overhead in the early light.

He wouldn't look at Ellen.

Charlotte lay on the couch, nestling the phone in whispered utterance that sounded out like pain—but she was smiling when she hung up the phone and waved a notepad and said, "This is my trip to Boston, Gra-mum. I'll leave it here for now." Kleenex crud (there were tears, of course), two pencils, a notepad and numbers on the notepad, numbers turned fat with writing over and over them, and also her name and the boyfriend's name, cars, flights, a small stack of pennies—kid wreckage.

Charlotte said, "I'll be right back," and the house sighed behind her when she closed the door.

He had a daughter once . . . but to think of her now was a grief, and yet he thought of her.

"Jimmy go downstairs and tell him he has to go home now." Ellen holds out his robe, but he shrugs off finding slippers though the floor is oddly cold and aches his legs. And then the sounds he hears—he should go back to bed or bang a chair against the floor or call out darkly, "It's late!" But he walks downstairs nonetheless, and he sees her in a way a father shouldn't.

It sickened him to think how little good his health had done her.

the moon is no mother

I am so tired of how the women are
their heads shrunken on the tips of sticks
and the light only they believe to be fire
why do they spend their sadness on trajectories?
the air is ill
silences live in it like passengers crammed in a car
here the mushrooms grow like toes in the dirt
how I hate women's grief
those sunken-eyed children thought to be lost
the ones with the grubbiest halos
the men always an angle in the distance
an exhumed cauliflower is a baby's brain
smoke exits the ashes
like hair undone before a mirror

Can You Help Me

it's so desperate the way she looks—too tan, too blonde
to be hanging out at Costco asking for change

hard lined face, she's been at it a while, drugs, poverty, who knows
what else

California sun gives false health
it's the inner death, the one we all avoid

that's taken her under, that takes you under
as you turn away "Not today"

But returning to the car, you hand her an orange,
the one you'd intended to eat for breakfast

and in the act, for an instant, you're not subject to flood of light and
shopping carts

morning sun too much to bear, honestly, too much

Ralph's, Lake and Lincoln, Late Night

Hispanic check-out woman ignores my items while ringing them up,
    Hey, homie
are those your tortillas? she says to the guy behind me.

No, he says. *You working late every night?*

Every night. Three kiwi (for a dollar) float on the conveyer belt and the canned soup.

Shit, he says.

This invisibility goes deeper than customer service.
She imagines my life to be easy, the life she deserves.

I want to tell her, I know what it's like to be caught,
to do whatever is necessary.

Homie, don't care. He has his six-pack and energy to flirt.
I hide behind *People* until the bag boy says *Paper or plastic*?

Half-smile as if the way we ignored each other

answers anger stilled as flies in the cold, no longer personal.

Alley, Indiana Avenue

Sparrows on the phone wires like abacus beads

over the Venice alley, mangled baby carriage garbage men can't take
(mysteriously bicycle-locked to chain link fence)

black can line up of issued trash and blue recycle bins—order for the
    eye

Del Taco wrapper, a used condom like sausage casing

Some days there's beauty in it, the desolate no
one cares atmosphere—some care, plant roses, yellow angels in their
    yard

Feng Shui bamboo to hide behind from the less desirables
The known drug addict down the street has sworn off heroin

He might even try N.A., if not today, tomorrow
and what's a few drinks, everyone drinks or smokes

Venice 13 has tagged a garage with graffiti—modern hieroglyph

You can almost sense the Pacific in the way clouds form, boisterous
    and absolute

Meanwhile, cars down Lincoln Boulevard *whizz*
fast as spitballs from the chute of a straw

Unwanted *Pennysaver*, Starbucks cup, the carpet cleaning coupon
    tossed
each individual gesture—a consequential whole.

Alte Romerstrasse, Dachau 2001

"Out of the depths I cry to you, O God . . ."
Psalm 130, Hebrew Bible

the worst part was not the pictures of men in jail-suits, hands tied
behind their backs,
hung from the wrists, dangling inverted—

that dislocates your shoulders, said my mother; or the accounts of
medical experimentation—
another man's scalp cut off so as tourists we saw his cranial matter,
wormy, bloodless bald monk's cap

and still more, a floating woman—clothed in a tank of cold water

an experiment designed to test the body's resistance to extreme tem-
peratures,

or the crematorium, empty—the un-noted dead, *this room was
never used as an actual crematorium*
the trench where people were lined up and shot

the worst part was not the recessed eyes of the starving of the sleep-
ing quarters like stalls
or the fact the Museum started with a history of the Nazi party and
not an apology, not a prayer

In renovation, said the sign

how we couldn't find our balance, *this happened in your lifetime*,
I say to my mother and we are stunned with mutual denial—the
ground beneath us opening up

as if the mouths of the dead want to speak in the dark, want the
odd silence of *beautiful* spring

to shimmer like a vigil—not drug us with oblivion and light

we are cold in our coats and gloves, the leftover snow in patches
    across the ground
inside the Church of Reconciliation a few votives burn, little teacups
    of spirit

the worst part was, not what was said, but what wasn't—how some-
    thing so dark
could still live a little, part scar, part shame, entirely evil

how you had to listen hard to hear *history* above the blare of the
    present.

See-Through Dream

In the dream we are all naked; a naked man mistakes me for a
man.
"Are you wood or bush?"
"Wood," he answers looking at my genitals.
"I am a woman," I insist
closing the screen door behind me.

A dream where so much is see-through.

When I wake up, I feel more male, not *her*;
tired of the desire to make a home, make babies,
give love to God's creatures, defer power, be sweet.

All fire, ready to take and not worry if it offends.

(you hate cats?)

In the dream my ex-husband is heavier than I remember like a
wrestler (code
for struggle I get it)—
glad to see me.

Near the 14 Street subway in the park, where the Farmers' Market
is held, a
stocky model, all in white
slides down a covered board intended to simulate snow—the seat
of her pants
wet like a kid's,
thong showing through.

His apartment looks good. Jocko doesn't chase his cat—but the
cat hides.
(you hate cats?)

"I'll always love you,"
he says—"but I don't want to touch you."

My two Indian friends (from India) have just appeared and the
three of them
make dinner plans
without me.

Consensual Silence

in the dream I fear men but say nothing—reduction of disagreement—self with self and not the world
at large, two spiders—bodies bulbous as cocktail onions hang from the shelves
like the consensual silence inside me—

small girl, small girl, girl whose only infraction is *being in the way* of that rage

later: the world like a bright jewel, rain on branch—
dropped

If Fame Were Not an Accident, and History a Distillation of Rumour

Raw light, erase the north side of the neighbors' house
so I can see inside this morning,
see all motion edged in shame,
see its married prophets arguing in robes of flame.
The waves of heat come billowing. Ow, it hurts.
But cold wind, blow through the windows into them.
Cold turns the volume down on everything
but thin sounds. Sharpens door slams into sparks,
freeze-dries footsteps over snow to squeaks.
It's not that cold, but with the wind they say
it feels like zero out. They (we) say since yesterday
a man who was married has lost half his name;
before the hyphen there's now a pause
we will all have to try and remember
not to say. Almost hoarded,
almost brought to the lips, brought there and moving them,
just not to words:
we've become, since yesterday, alien to ourselves.
Another man we know embezzled—
it's daytime, he's switched off the lights.
The story has him calling up a pornographic image
on his computer screen where he leaves it
all day to be discovered by women
breasting the vasty deep of dusk
with coffee, letters to be signed. The covenant—
that they too feel shame.
Wasn't his taking the money enough for us?
The cold yellow-green of computer light:
we hold it like a firefly inside a jar.
The snow that was melting down the roof
has frozen in its tracks
to ice dams and enormous gnarled icicles

each with a gothic silence stuck inside.
If gossip were the cold wind blowing through town
it might release us all
from the little gusts and flurries.
Gossip, are we on the verge
of your vast exteriority? The porch steps
are shoveled and mute, the catprints leading over snow
are suddenly gone, as if the cat had been lifted
cleanly out of itself by a hawk so ravenous
it left no trace of blood. Oh man
it looks cold out even from here,
though when the heat comes on
it comes on like the final exhalation of a Wal-Mart Store.
That's not forgiveness. That's not everlasting light.
Neighbors, close the curtains so your bodies
shine; then we'll close our eyes and seek out the paths of heat.

I Finde in a Boke Compiled to this Matere an Olde Histoire

. . . reading Bill's starred copy of History

Measured by human reading time, they are old stars. Something that belongs not to the past but to us though I wasn't there yet. Left-handed stars, each begun and ended at its radiating upper point. Often the lines don't meet, the star stays open a crack. Or the line continues through itself just below the space it started and the star opens up again. I don't want to make too much of this, just everything. *Historein, historia. To inquire.* Greek and Roman and Midwestern history. Athens, Florence, Des Moines. See *Weid—*. To see. Sometimes a star nearly flies or shrugs out of itself, sometimes there's a pock at the first/last point, where the pencil first hit the page or where it lifted off, which was it, twenty years ago. "Almost 80 of the poems in *History* are new," Mr. Lowell is quoted as saying on the back of the book. Before we went inside the house on Hol Hi Avenue, we wanted to buy it just because it bordered on a quiet with trees. And because of the name of the street. Once inside we didn't like the house; we adored the view. *View, vista, vision* are some important derivatives. *Survey, idea, history, story.* And *penguin* from the Welsh *gwyn—white.* The page of my Jane Austen was filled with snow, the only sound the clinking of her bracelets. Where I came from you don't write in your books. He is part of his time, she is part of hers, though time gets dark at the top, I can't see into it. It's OK, I can hear him in the kitchen chopping kale exactly now. No, it is the smell of onions drifting to me. *Evident, interview.* Entre, between, plus voir, to see. A history isn't windows and trees. To write truly the history of last week, we would meet, some he and she, light years ago in Des Moines, Witmer Pond, put our bodies on in a light wind, put on all they have to say under one of the trees, open the book—not the trees, don't carve names on them—and start writing all over it.

Scar

There was a certain blank spot within her where she went to when she needed to do something she otherwise wouldn't have. That was how she accomplished the tattoo. As she moved about the world during such times, no one could have guessed what she was thinking. She did not speak to herself, that was key.

"There," she said, pointing to her shoulder blade. "Right there."

"You're sure?" the tattoo artist had asked.

She nodded.

It took a full hour. The design flourished; the blood was wiped away. A black hawk. He had told her often that she was his black hawk, beautiful, soaring, a little ominous. They had seen many of these birds on their daylight excursions, and made love under their halted flight. Now, he would know for sure.

The tattoo was more expensive than she had imagined it would be, and she had to put it on her charge card.

The design's scabs slowly sloughed up from and off her skin, left glowing ink behind. It itched terribly for weeks. She was able, for once in her life, to control herself. That showed something, she was sure. A new strength.

He had told her that he would phone her in a month, and they would talk then. Until that time, he asked her, he would need to be by himself, with his wife and kids, to try and sort things out. See if there was anything left there. It wasn't an easy decision, she must know that. She had wanted to know if there was any hope, if he still thought about her that way. He still thought about her all the time. He didn't know yet. Yes, she told him, she would wait. The next day, she went to the tattoo parlor.

By the time he phoned, the design had healed. Permanent. In the bathroom mirror, she often studied the design and found that she liked it. Sometimes she laughed at herself for having done something so rash. What was she thinking? She hadn't been. Still, the tattoo added something to her that hadn't been there before. She stroked the tattoo in bed before she fell asleep, and pretended that her hand was his.

' ' '

On the phone, his voice was wrong. Yes, he still wanted to see her. They had to talk. Yes, everything was fine. It was best if they talked that day.

She left work unexplained and met him at the winery gardens where they had first kissed. He sat in the gazebo of the gardens, alone, without a picnic lunch. He had come in the station wagon, not the convertible. She knew right then that it was over. All over but the shouting. She couldn't, however, resist the shouting. She had something to show him.

"Well," she said.

No. It wouldn't work. He did love his wife. They had so much together. He couldn't throw it all away. There were the kids. There were bigger things at stake. His family would be his family forever; there was no changing that. He could not see her any more. It was hard for him, he hoped she understood. He would always love her, always have a place for her in his heart. It had been the best five months of his life.

Then he stopped talking.

"But..." she said, and he shook his head at her.

Nothing more to say.

"What about this then?" she said. She stripped off her shirt and turned her shoulder to him. "What do I do with this?"

He said nothing at first, but his eyes were wide, softened. He reached out to touch it, but she pulled away.

He wanted to know why she had done it. Had she lost her mind?

"You said forever," she said.

"It's beautiful," he said. "Can I touch it, please?"

"No."

In the dusty summer light, high noon, the tattoo glowed, impervious to the day. Inescapable.

He went to the station wagon and came back with a bag full of cards and letters. He wanted her to have them; he could not afford to keep them. She tossed the bag of paper on the ground.

"What about Terry?" she asked.

When they had first slept together, he had told her about his first affair, several years previous. He and Terry, another co-worker, had been flirting for months, and had once kissed in the Xerox room after hours. But it was mild, harmless. Until he ran into her at a bar one afternoon on the way home from work. Terry was there with some friends, but she came to him and took him to a booth in the back, where they sat together with their backs to the bar, talking and drinking for a couple of hours. It was late and he had to go. She wanted to know where he was going. Home, of course. Terry wanted him to come home with her. He couldn't. She pulled away from him in the booth and turned to face him. She lifted her skirt above her thighs. An enormous, vivid tattoo of a red dragon covered the inside of her left thigh.

He didn't get home until four that morning. His wife was bolt awake, but said nothing when he climbed into bed. He had stopped off at an all-night diner on the way home and devoured a plate of french fries to cover his scent. He and Terry saw each other off and on for over a year.

"That was different," he told her. "I never intended to be with her forever. She knew that. She already had the god damned tattoo. Why did you do that?"

They sat in silence for a long time. She looked up at one point and started to say something, but he shook his head at her.

He went into the tasting room to use the facilities, and while he was gone, she left. She walked past his station wagon on the way to her car and scratched the entire length of the passenger side with her keys, knowing that he would not see it for a while, hoping that his wife would discover the mark. She knew the exposed metal would rust. He'd have to have a complete paint job.

Months later, in bed, her new lover asked her about the tattoo. What did it mean?

She told him that she got it a long time ago, for someone else, but that hadn't worked out. But she'd been smart in her choice of designs and chose something that was meaningful to her. She was the black hawk, soaring, impervious. Stationed above it all, waiting for the prey.

Her new lover was amazed; the tattoo looked so fresh.

The man who had done it to her was very good, she said. He promised her that it would stay vivid, fully colored, sharply etched forever.

Subterranean

To move in a woman, he says, is to move
underneath

that place on the map where the body gives in
& the mind shuts off (long gasp

that sounds like sorrow.) It's no crime to want to live

where the sun beats down
with the conviction of a drug

& it isn't a crime to love

the pitch black curve of the ever elusive tunnel,
the apocalyptic white of her thigh—

the swing of hair, long past jasmine and
on its way to blithe.

Long ago I also reached to touch a woman's hair.
It scared me half

to death. Its rustling, oceanic
dreaming.

Blind Alley

Lilies; those charming imposters.
In the adamantine daze

of the low slung sun, they tried
to convince you.

You always fell in love with manmade things—

The future hovered,
in taut, industrial darkness. The world at large

stood up, in dumb applause.

How they beckoned; relentless, forgiving.
The sound of another summer,

bottoming out.

Wingspan

That's the trouble with love, she thinks,
it's parenthetical.

Her one true vein is in her upper thigh, no map

he can follow. Notice her exhale;
it's a little bit longer than his. Still,

he gets her down to what she wants: her whittled list.

Once, she licked his Christ-like inner wrists
with her own brand of un-

restraint, akin to terror. She knows one thing
and likes to think it, hard:

the birds evicted

from their troubled path of flight. His lupine kiss.

South of Morgantown

In the other day of the other life in a space south of Morgantown
it goes on. It continues there;
you can't see the kids but their voices float like a spray
up through the pines. Those hundreds of pines all so calm,
studying how to get some sun and rain in useful amounts
for getting tall and what else, taller and expressing
boughs outward every way. This continues there
south of Morgantown and on a hot day
all the kids go over to Lake Floyd
along about three p.m. They ride down Flinderation Road
and they drink some Pepsi or beer depending on their age
and jump around in Lake Floyd a while
and dry off on the rocks, maybe play cards.
We feel
a stretching in ourselves toward them, those kids down there
or is it toward the lake itself or toward the calm of those pine trees
because our life, this one, seems like what happens when
the fine clear simple thing is somewhere else. Those kids ride
far down Flinderation Road out of sight and when their voices come
like spindrift of hot haze the force of it is the way we don't see them,
we don't see the sweat on the freckles, the dirt in the sweat,
the blue bubble gum and the fatuous small cruelties or
blind enforcements of loneliness; and so they can be
in that other day down there the sense of what clear fine thing
we've failed to keep.
Anne, Anne,
sit near me on the rock while we dry in the sun.
Anne, those droplets on your legs are shining so quietly!
What is the song she hums as if to herself but letting us hear?
It is "Dream a Little Dream of Me."

Rome of Dream

Down the long hill
down the crumbling cracked stairs
and the next set of dark cracked stairs that curve the other way
down and between imperviously old walls
down I go to reach—to find—

Is it a woman I am to seek? Or is that a banal reduction?
Do I have the map

The cars will magically avoid me if I keep moving
but if I pause they will break my legs—this must mean
that some central power desires motion

I am to have an experience
there is a summoning—the summoning has the eyes of a woman
who is just turning the corner

These are the next stairs—steep—at the bottom
on a parked motorino a young woman sits astride her man:
How do they inhabit such clear plain desire?
Forget her thighs
Check the map
Check it again—do not lose the map

Why have I crossed three bridges? There is only one river on the map

That saxophone man from Ponte Sisto him with the dark red face
he is not following me—why would he be following me
I only have 20,000 lire—no wait it's 200,000 lire—there is a difference
remember the difference, 200,000 lire is too much for one pizza
To be robbed would be to be proven unfit for the dream

This street just changed its name it was Via dei Banchi Vecchi and
    now
it's Via dei Cappelari but I have no proof that this change comes from

malice
Most of the streets are on the map but not all of the streets—wait
where is the map? Not in this pocket—not in this pocket
not in this one I already checked the other pocket Oh here is the way
this is
the way our friend led us that day—but now it is dark
and the street here is so narrow it must soon cease
and yet here behind me come three motorinos—
their goal is to crush my toes without noticing—
if they don't notice then it is not malice it is only the mistake of my
presence
but if I move fast enough to be invisible—

Here is a piazza: everything is peaceful in a piazza that must be what
the word means
piazza—peace
but is this the one—I wanted the Piazza of Experience—

She must be going there, that one, with the high heels, I could fol-
low her and find it
but she is gone clicking across the black cobblestones
No there she is—or her sister—why does she never glance at me
I am invisible—is this good because I am free or bad because I am
lost
I went the wrong way on Via dei Serpenti
so now I must do everything differently
and faster—the other way—

faster the other way
Thank God there are no beautiful women on this street
People were tortured on this spot one thousand years ago
That little bus the 116 is probably the answer, the secret answer
but it has swerved away—but look
this is a way down these steps down—these steps were waiting in the
dark
exactly where someone was tortured two thousand years ago
his head forced down into hot oil—BUT if I keep walking fast I won't
be caught

Caught for what? For being free—or lost? Look now if I take Via del Boschetto
not to Termini not to that place of trees where the starlings are insane at dusk
take Via del Boschetto to Via degli Zingari—and be not distracted by Vicolo Sambuco
and veer from Piazza degli Zingari into Via Clementina then—
if I turn at the right moment I will see
her—
who?—her—through a shop window: she will be at the desk
leaning intelligently toward a computer screen and not glancing up
but I cannot watch her for long because I would become visible
and when you are visible you can be acted upon, they can speak to you
in a river of syllables and sell you a jacket—do I want a new jacket?
But I was looking for a certain piazza

wait look there is the statue the dark statue of the hooded man:
he means something dark and rich with pain for someone—others
far gone but not for me! I am not caught in this dark stone silence I'm
breathing—breathing here in Campo dei Fiori
though I've misplaced my map.

Rise And Fall

Around midnight I hear a woman singing something down in the alley so I go to the window to see what I can see. Seconds later, Elias comes to the staircase window on his side of the alley and two of the loneliest people ever to don PVC undergarments find themselves blinking at each other across the great divide. Tonight the divide is a column of drizzle and a lot of bad feeling.

It's my mother singing. The song is *Whiter Shade Of Pale*. What with her no longer incipient senility and her no longer distensible bladder ("It's like a bag of pebbles, Mona," my father tells me), Mom takes an age to finish peeing and pull up her tights.

When she gets to the last line of the chorus, I look again at Elias and, on account of the headlights of the cop car that's just now nosing into the alley, his face *does* turn a shade of pale that's whiter than is normal for a thirty-seven-year-old fitness fanatic. So Mom is peeing in drains and I'm looking across at my estranged husband, whose face tells me that I'm stuck in the same horrible white-out headlight glare as him, and that yes, a relationship based on timorous butt-slapping and a shared career in constitutional law was never going to survive New York City in the dissolute last days of the American Empire.

Gallant

When a nice boy has deliberately overstepped the mark and your daughter is wailing like the end of time just occurred inside her body, I think you're in the right if you run to the window and climb down that drainpipe like the hero in a movie. I can't be Ms. Lilith Fair all the time, can I, so it's actually fine with me if you make a unilateral decision to chase Alvin Hoyt across the lawn, knock his legs out from under him and smash him really hard in the face. Because what's intolerable, Dad, is if you stand in the doorway playing with your keys and asking a lot of perfectly *sensible* questions.

Who

You know when you're walking down the street and you see someone walking in the opposite direction on the other side of the road, except that you can't see his face because the two of you happen to have synchronised your speeds in such a way that he's partially hidden behind a lamppost, which seems to move *with* him as the two of you continue on your respective ways, and you're a bit anal so you keep looking because it'd be nice just to catch a quick glimpse of his face before you pass each other, but although the lamppost isn't obscuring him any more, you now find yourself looking at the back of his head as he walks away, and as a result you're tempted just to cross the road and walk after him and be in casual pursuit of him, because if you don't just satisfy your curiosity while you have the chance, perhaps you'll regret that you walked on, and you know you shouldn't give in to these impulses but you also don't want to end up going mad again, this time because you couldn't stop thinking about some stranger's eternally featureless face?

Qattara Depression

Montgomery may continue to resemble a ferret: permission is granted. Field-Marshals may poke their legs into jodhpurs and (of necessity, I think) be courageous, awkward and rather silly, all at the same time. Any fellow may do as he pleases, Artie, just as long as he prosecutes the bloodshed in double-quick fashion. Is there a Christmas any more? I mean as a feeling in people's hearts, or even something to peer at from a distance? One gets thoroughly despondent about the length of time our boys take to murder their boys, and vice versa. It's a wicked thing to say, but we've become mathematicians, even the bumpkins among us, and we're nothing if not cynical.

Art, what a disgusting to-do it's been. I shan't ever forget any of it, and I think probably I shall go mad in spells like a west-country Sassoon. You'll say a prayer for me, won't you? And in turn I promise to use the mind's eye to reprise your face every now and then. Your gruesome face will hove into view and I'll punch it on the nose!

Tonight is Alexandria. I plan to let several soft young women into the shell of my heart, so to speak, and I don't intend to be too much of a good sort about it. While you're kneeling in that pew, perhaps you should pray for the survival of the Gentleman?

But does God still exist? God hasn't been seen in months.

Closed for the Season

What to say next? You were ill.
Pushing your pen in circles

on the corner of a napkin.
I was trying to remember—

five years, I guess, since I'd seen you—

newly arrived in Chicago,
in love. Now

you were waving away the gloom.

You: Tegretol and Clorazil.

Our knees almost touching
at the counter at Starbucks–

not you as I knew you:

even your urban radar down.

Rings True

It hangs on, but how? Your kindness

hangs on.

(Economically fragile and technologically backward.)

It turns dumb documents
(like this photo

of a tree-lined road)

into something storied. Coagulated
in thousands of pages.

        (Digital erasure forgotten as foretold.
        Computer enhancement abandoned.)

        Props change, sets change,
your kindness does not change.

From title to candle-lit coda—

(bombproof) (complex)—

        swimming in a sea of raised fists...

        your kindness is a curiosity.
        It hangs on. (It rings true).

In Church

How many ways are there to fail?

The giant scrim of my own personality—
shot fat goose—perpetually in the way,

blocking out The Good.

Is there anybody who can vouch for you?

Church is a Wax House:
paints, tints, glittering fabrics

and shiny stones. And not only

through the soft focus of cataracts,
corrected lenses,

and maximum amplification,

does it appear to matter –

hence my pew-mates seem happy
to call this home. "Happy"

might not be right. But out of the social,

because of their histories,
there is something—"home" feels close.

If only I weren't so over-ripe,
I'd sense it, too, I suppose…

I mean even if I'm open to what's next—
the greasy kneeler, the guilty thought,

the candle flickering as if to say
I'd be the first to admit things are tough –

how do I make that minute last?

Perhaps I need to turn the screws,
make myself care more—

or care more deeply. Will this, in turn,
feel like a kiss?

    Only not so human. A self-kiss:

more casket than rice.

Jacque Cousteau After Becoming a Fish Visits Melville Who Has Become the Sea

To save three California gray whales locked under ice in arctic seas,
Scientists
Play whale love tapes to lure them to safety.

An intelligence is moving under water.
Irenic songs.
Minds moving beneath us,
Trying to touch us.
Teachers.
They wait—
The way light waits in stone before it is diamond.
Just words tapping against something
Hard and frozen.

I stand inside this season's first falling.
The air is growing solid around me.
I can't believe the thickness of this ceiling.
I scrape my mouth
Against it. I can't breathe.
I listen for the sound
Of something fierce and familiar.

We are always reaching.
I reach for a child
Falling down a hole inside me.

I reach for a man to save him
And pull out fire. When I get my hand back,
It is screaming. I hold this burning before me,
And it is me.

Ed McMahon Meets Marcel Duchamp Through the Mails

I just received a letter from Ed McMahon
saying I won $10,000,000. Not bad.

I once knew a woman and we sent holes
to each other through the mail.
White sheets of paper with circles cut into them.
That's when I fell in love with the great mystery of the mail.

Ed McMahon looks happy
but it also appears as if he has a dirty face.
I wouldn't want someone handing me $10,000,000
if he had a dirty face.

They found a hundred pounds of undelivered mail
burning under a Chicago viaduct.
There is always the danger
that whatever we say ends up on fire.

When I was in sixth grade
I was in the slow class
with a number of older students
who'd failed quite a few times.
I tried to say a mistake had been made,
but no one listened.

I sat behind a girl named Barbara,
and she sat across from this older boy
named Richard.
He would take this thing out of his pants
and lay it on his leg.
I had never seen anything like it.
It seemed to have a life of its own.
At first, Barbara didn't want to look,
but then he'd sing a song for her.
Or maybe the song was for this thing

that moved in his lap.
A few years later he was serving
a sentence for stealing mail
from the Post Office.
I don't know if these two things are connected.

I feel sorry for Ed McMahon.
It is as if he never had a life.
If I won the ten million,
I would invite him over.
I'd have him sit next to me on the couch and chat.
Maybe I'd invite other people over
and we'd chat together.

I go to the mailbox as if it were a tabernacle,
as if this great mysterious river of things were coming toward us
and this is where it stopped.

        Ed McMahon asks, "Will I be awarding you
Ten Million Dollars? It could all depend
on what you do right now." I feel
the pressure. What happens
            if I don't do anything?

And then I'd like you to explain this:
I got this thing in the mail that said UFOs
are from volcanoes. According to this, UFOs are really
volcanic material that travels thousands of miles.

What are they trying to do:
take away our hope?

A woman and I once sent holes through the mails.
All we wanted was for each other to fill them.
And now I write a letter to Barbara.
I don't think it was right—the singing and all.

It begins: Barbara, I'm suspicious
about this $10,000,000 thing.
It appears that Ed McMahon is lying or at least
exaggerating.

I try to say a mistake has been made,
but no one listens.

I hear they found a mail truck in NYC
with this burning mail in the back.
All the bills, all the faces of Ed McMahon,
all the catalogues of the 10,000,000 things
that keep us sad. And the words—
maybe 10,000,000 words—flickering, flashing.
These fire words. These flying words.
They fill these holes inside us
with something that feels like hope.

Blake Watches Mr. Milton's Angels Burning in Madame Curie's Hair

The burning lady of Toronto burns in her building.
Her dress ablaze, she spreads to the hallway

Of her apartment, knocking on the doors where some
Reluctantly answer. Smelling the sizzle of her ribbons,
A man opens his door a slit. "Spring must be here,"

He says to his wife. The burning lady burns;
Her lips spark. A woman looks through her peephole,

The burning lady blazing on the other side. "Ah,
The lucrative light of the noon. Isn't everything amazing?"
Another opens his door to the theory of fire. Still

Another to the beginning of time. The ashes
Of her housecoat singe a trail in the rug. A fat man

Watches the heart of a dancer bursting. Her shoes
Turn into smoke. Another sees an angel with flaming
Wings or sees a sinner about to repent. He can't

Tell looking through the monocle on his door.
While the burning lady stands in her combustible shoes,

A woman watches Dresden under a night of shooting stars.
The next time you open your door, a woman
Will be standing there, burning like a ruby.

I want you to believe this. She will be burning,
Burning, burning. And you will see something else.

H. D. Imagiste and Edward Lorenz Discover a Butterfly in Brazil

Still, when you wake,
A bird in Paraguay
Turns into the color
Of your pupils. The story
We tell to find our joy
Starts in the story we tell
To express our sorrow. OK?
A cat's paw lands
In a carpet: an earthquake
In Quebec. An eel lights up
A small portion of the ocean:
An electrical storm
In Managua.

You want the child
Remembered, resurrected
In a thousand places.
Any child.
It is like opening a chrysalis
To find our faces.
It is like opening a TV
To find our memories inside
Replaced with light.
Seventeen things become
Extinct each hour
While the lake carries
Time in its belly.

Somewhere in the universe
There is a slight omission,
A trivial alteration of a fact.
Some word altered in a poem
Ineluctably changes the course
Of events. When someone

Removes a rainbow from a head
In Moscow, new colors
Fall over Madrid. I think
Women all over the planet
Give birth to the same child.

can't meet the wind

let's see: i can't walk into your
apartment because you have the flu /
can't meet the wind because the field
is so wet i would sink in mud /
can't make the sight of the deer without
maybe spooking them / the dot before
my eyes / the rain on the windshield /
simple gray band of a ring / i bridge
a very tired face she has from working
too long and drinking too much and now
her farmer uncle is staying with her
for two days / it is her complaint
not mine /

Poem

What is that one long line of winter
across the page - the sound that is nowhere
but now is in someone - something there, at the page's
edge - a field with snow in some reserved but reversed

relationship to the field, so that the fences impose
themselves on the page like words or sometimes a foreign
line - superimpose themselves on the page like words
or a person who has gone crazy with words -

silence and popularity are the same thing -
the person with the lamp is the person with the snow -
the person with one is the person with the other -
many and few are the same proposition -

a word you used once in a mistaken move
in a mistaken house - under a mistaken sky -
a word with someone already in it -
and there was no room for you -

and you knew this
but you could not stop.

10/20/99

I'm looking for Tom Clark's comment on Robert Creeley
: page 27
"point of
exhaustion"

so goes my note
Actually my note goes in hand
Clark on
Creeley page

27

"point of
exhaustion"

The underlining
is light—my 1 in Creeley
almost has a little head on its left
—the 7 in 27 is a Europena 7 with a slash through it
(and now I see there is also a line underneath the 7—to its left

7

I don't know why I would
even talk about this except that
the note like many fascinates me
as an accidental thing - not intended

to be of interest
and my maybe not of interest!
but here I am with it
and here I have also asked a question

way above it
(Where is that, Professor Poetry?)
the question is
Duhamel reaches no
point of
exhaustion?

The other side of the note is interesting too
—it reads Thief poem—then in another half

woman-
in-bus
station-
White Light

there are lines on this small page too
which lend it some other slightly interesting quality
I really didn't want to locate the Clark remark
because I read Creeley in this kind of endless way

in the fact of many hours and places
in my life
and I have always found Clark's take on him
more than of interest

really onto something
and I want to find this and know this
but in another way I want it all to be
signposts which it really is

for me
signposts
constants
no givens

just takes and retakes
and the movie is this way
and the movie is that
and the material on the cutting room

floor is very interesting too
and I abide in it among it all
as I can and want to

Untitled

Why not the infantile
frame—a window like
a cell, an if-black-
and-white frame the cell

is biological, memory
maybe also—the past
is, is. Present too,
too. Certain behaviors

must be like old moons
of forgotten planets—
and this isn't to say
one or I or you or we

are perhaps helpers or passive
or victims. It's just
the odd arrangement
which keeps changing.

As the Invisible Man Though Less Visible

I am the youngest of six children. Astrologically, Saturn returns into a person's house on a 29-year cycle. It's a havoc wreaker. My siblings have all passed through their Saturn house. But I haven't. I'm the youngest. They have found their special purposes. I haven't.

We go to the movies together and get 12 seats even though I'm not married, not even dating anyone except Elijah the Prophet. I met Elijah at a Passover Seder. He sat next to me because I didn't have a date. Few people at the party, in fact, no one, could see him. Elijah the Prophet is invisible.

At the movies, when my family gets tired of the tub of popcorn, they put it in Elijah's seat and I pretend I'm not too bothered that its always my boyfriend who has to be the stand-up man, has to hold the greasy container.

After the movie my oldest sister tries talking to Elijah. "Were you scared when the bad guy was hiding in the pantry?" she asks him. But Elijah doesn't answer.

When we get home Elijah is quiet. He is still quiet when we go to bed. I think, quietly, maybe he is receiving his prophesy. Maybe his prophesy has something to do with my special purpose. Eventually, most every night, I get tired of waiting for him to tell me what that special purpose might be. Most every night it feels like I am alone even when I am with him.

But then I think I hear him say, "Don't worry baby," or, "Tonight is the night we eat reclining," or, "I don't care if you're not Jewish." I exhale. Never holding or beholding him, it is lonely work.

One of my sisters calls. She wants to set me up on a blind date. After some thought I decline the offer. "I already have a boyfriend," I tell her. I already have a blind date. Though my date is not blind, invisible is near blind, like a neighbor. My sister won't call back for a few weeks. She will spend that time throwing her arms in the air, saying, "I tried to help her." That is part of her special purpose.

"Elijah?" I ask in the middle of the night. "Will you hug me?"

I wait. I think I feel something.

"Elijah?" I ask. "Is that you?" After waiting awhile longer I begin to realize that chances are Elijah went to the kitchen for a glass of water and once there he was distracted by the window. He went to investigate something shimmering outside, something like neon, or gold, or streetlight or communication with the divine.

After being in love with Elijah the Prophet I would find it impossible to return to dating mortals. But still I think about how one day we'll probably break up, then I picture it, having a normal husband and maybe children. I can see how, at the breakfast table, I would torture my mortal husband with what Elijah has taught me: the truth of our pure loneliness.

And that is why I love Elijah. He never tries to cover up this truth. I say to him, "Pass the ice tea," or, "Do you want to dance?" or "If you love me, reveal yourself," and his answer is always the same, each word of it invisible.

Poem

Sometimes, after, its small fire still

thrumming just under my skin, I
am in awe of this self, sensing once more

I am not what I would think, not body (*early winter light holding against late day chill*);

not the end of this one conception;

but the nature of awe
and the nature of doubting it.

Discourse

And I said to him, we are continuous,
And whatever the self is, it is never
As we would consider, so I don't believe the possibility
Of speaking too much of it; and he says to me,
Continuous, exactly, with what?

What about the body: something is always pulling at it
—gravity, responsibility, the life after this one.

My siblings and I don't speak to each other
As much as we used to. When one of us calls, we talk
About the care of our father, our aunts, and then
We talk about the children. In the pauses, we acknowledge
How different from each other we've become,
And each of us somehow considers how much
We miss the way things briefly were.

The Point of the Story

That next morning, a little depressed, I said, Self,
Don't you finally get tired of yourself?
And the answer was obvious, but not absolute,
Which is, of course, just like a self.
So I countered, What's your point?, uncovering

The whole other realm of questions and conjectures,
Only a few of which make sense.
Over dinner, my friend who was writing another novel
Had said she thought the narrative impulse was too much
With us in the end, even when

We move toward fracture, write towards nonsense.
I agreed with her, lamenting that I sometimes feel
I only tell one story,
And there is always that other side.
As for all of the other stories, Well, you can imagine.

A book has its cover, its author
Probably not a good judge. Despite my best efforts,
I keep coming back to talking to myself.
It's harder and harder to finally tell
Just what I'm saying back.

My Personal Epistemology

I don't know what to believe, sometimes.

There are a few people I have known
With whom we knew what the other was thinking,
And sometimes we were thinking of each other
For exactly the same reason. We knew not to dismiss this as only
 chance.
I would know something was very wrong with my friend, for
 instance,
And when I called him the first thing he would say was,
I knew it would be you.

I believe the proof of an idea about the world lies
In the world of the personal, and the personal is evidence of being
 meaning-
Fully in the world.
I believe the truth of language lies in who is speaking.
I don't know if knowledge and belief are speaking the same thing.

I often believed that, wherever in the world
I was, I would know the exact moment each of my parents died,
But I don't know why
That didn't really happen with my mother
And what that will mean about my father.

Because I was not saved, my family began to worry
About my eternal soul. I told them I didn't believe as they did,
And what seemed to hurt us most
In all this was what we all now knew.

Intertext

I throw a rose on the street
and wait for the car (with you in it).

My rose (bruised)
prettifying the oil slicks

and you in the car, blond, fast
like solar wind (chasing dawn).

The Pillars of Community

Two leather money belts
hung around the bony hips.

They are like illness and joy
(how fat, how frantic),

dirty blond who smells armpits,
metal mouth that eats hambones.

Tectonics of the Imperceptible

I sit at my desk
waiting for you.

My heart (quick hound)
jumps to a memory:

blue land (your face),
around it the ocean of sleep.

Purpose and Extravagance

Wounded cross
and the statuary of broken angels,

I am open hearted.
Into me swing your wrecking

ball, your arraignments. I am yours
forever, plane-encrusted.

Rearview

I am alone (weep for me)
inside a car in Iowa.

My lover (hills on her mind)
has left me for an Alpinist

with money and muscles.
The mirror trembles (illusion).

Vegetable Tantra

You are okra to me,
you are vegetable stew,

seed pod, tomato
in a clandestine pot.

Remember how you nourished me
and I whirled like a dervish.

Paris Lure

Ripped into meaning the meaty night wears
itself like a joke overthrown. Mother
tongue! Help me. This attempt to disown her
murdered like an orange. Winter doesn't care
a lick. Absence is its home. I'm sick where
the journey leaves me broke. I can turn her
on. I can force her to find me, rupture
everything that's her belief. At the Gare
du Nord she's every woman and she's not.
Deep inside time, inside a lock I ride
a swallowed hold. Measure loss by what's caught
in the throat. Anonymous stranger, hide

your eyes. My entrails have clicked to ice. Christ,
the sky's after me. Paris breaks my mind.

Proof, no Proof

As a hurricane approaches a town
that is hideously bored, I owe you
reasons why I love you. It smells like blown
lust cultivated by absence's blue
geometries. Here is the honeycomb
answering you, poised like snowfall, done. Huge
silences escape the hollow moon's home
dissolved into failure. Nature's abuse
kisses us like stained-glass windows smashing
at our feet. The cathedral's over or
it never stood a chance like most passion.
I cannot do anything. The cracked roar

Of my heart means I'm blasted to the ground.
You who cannot weep cannot hear a sound.

Crush

You raise the wall of snow. You are snowfall
Demanding burial, suffocation.
The end of the world. I've been given all
You've never known. It's in the location
Of a severed field, the theory of speed,
frameless—A heart widened to ignore white
space, the landscape you revel in. To reach
you is impossible against the bite
of soundlessness. Mathematics will not help
this impasse. I love you in a moment
like this one. Listen to me drive it back
to America. We're in your car. Spent.

Your eyes don't lie. I know you inside me.
The way you know me. The buzz of a bee.

This Hard Earned Sleep

You don't know me. I'm a cliff, you can fall.
I blur you forget you, insert London.
I know how to breathe. Moon, I saw you (crawl
last night above the city) abandon
the universe for your own shape, near whole,
lobbed white like a proverb unwritten. Tight
out of black—A blossom burst—. Mirrored soul,
I want you back. Disturb my sleep. My right
to nothing is a murdered orange. The form
of shattered glass glued back. You are the first
to pause along this river. Are you torn
against the shore? After all, it's the worst

snow my heart has known. Drifts. Wind. Razor-ice.
My lips are cracked against disaster's price.

Sonnet Begun In A Pub in Edinburgh While Listening To A Traditional Scottish Band Perform: 30 August, 1998

My heart stops into me like rain presses
against the mind past blurred, nailed steel, breaking
glass, bagpipes splitting flesh. I find you. *Yes,*
I say, *I love you*, yes against time. Sink
into me, dismantle every bone O!
Break my spine in two into speed's halved core.
I wanted this, I want this, please don't
fade; fear, run, quit. I'll be your reservoir.
Your only whore. I can't speak. Shred me long
and hard. I've got your life inside my flesh.
I'm here to dance, to wreck my dead-end song.
You take me to the edge: a world made plush.

I've forgotten who I was before you
Moved me into a vision I can't undo.

Last Orders

Who in this tired room knows it's harder
than a search-light? How clearly you break me
from this tongue. I question what the murder
shut. The untamed hum, neurotic come-dream.
Christ, this bar's a black hole, a junk-yard, crap.
The two of us flung like a rip-tide wide
into a semi-automatic's lap.
Let's go then eat a plum until we're blind.
Don't joke about the theatre on time.
We possess the past, the party line is
you. Is there any fat to chew? My mind
is on you, whirly-gig. Pass the drink. Diz-

zy is the light askew. I long for you.
Here there everywhere. Love the one you lose.

There's Nothing So Bad Living Can't Fix It

I walked down the hall dreaming my dream
that had everything in it, even though
I didn't know what anything was
or what it was made of or how it worked
so I made up stories,
holding my own hand so I wouldn't be alone
if something terrible happened.

I was intimate with objects.
With the makers of objects through their works.
I was someone who'd someday make things
so a girl like me would never be lonely.

So she'd have a roof and food
and something to offer.
I'd gather up all she might need
and store it in a room marked
"Open When You're Free To Live."

I'd set her down a long path
with many burdens and obstacles
so she'd know her own strength,
become so familiar
she wouldn't be afraid of it.

One day she'd open the door a crack
and peek in
at the wonderful disorder
of her own room.

All her objects stained by disregard
had become beautiful,

all the sorrows she bore alone
had become the world.

Trepidar

Toward the moon's fullness
I begin to believe
my brothers & sisters & I
will learn to dance
we won't be afraid to love each other
it won't always be the same ricochet
from madness to clarity with no rest between

what each steals from the other
is the touch of our home planet
firm gentle nest

tonight the clouds are furious
the rain won't let up
the arc of the sky
sends down bolts of star cloth
we shiver under the moon
on wet grass
we are close but side by side, not facing
we use words but words sink to the ground
or flee toward some tree or bush
even physical touch between two skins
doesn't seem like the one we remember

I can speak for my brothers and sisters
who don't call when the moon is waning
only at its increase

tonight I think it may be full
maybe this is my last night of hope
what revelation will the darkness bring
that I'll carry with me back to the bright
high noon of shadows, what lost words
we strangers exchange
like metaphysical coins?

I hear the sound of universal currency
can I buy you with it?
can I own you, rub you smooth with my handling
know every part of you with every part of myself?

Once my mother held me inside her
I felt her voice, her walking
when she sang or made love or was hungry or peed
I was with her

At the new moon my heart bursts with love & anger
at the full I seek a receptacle and find there is none
with each change I've hardly mastered the last
I learn to breathe air then I'm staring at a carp

I don't get to work on time
I forget to comb my hair

none of this matters
except that I miss the certainty
of knowing one day I'd tear the membrane
on the other side
would be everyone I knew
only real, vivid
face to face

the rain gets louder
a car goes by
my left nostril drips
the rain gets even louder
now my hands remind me
I have a body & if my body dies

Broken Guitar

I have a broken guitar with four strings.
It makes nice music.
The wood is cracked and split, but it holds together.
I keep it near the altar of children.

I made this altar to honor the old journals
it covers. Imperfect self revealed
to remind me of where I came from.
Words threaded from page to page
show the madness and stupidity
that kept me alive. I strum the guitar
and listen to the sounds, a fool
but my flesh is fed.
I'd just like to thank the amino acids
that flew to earth on an asteroid
a long time ago.

Thank you, mysterious forces I express through being.
Thank you, mystery that I am.
Listen to my new song;

we carry the light and dark
in our transient boxes
that dissolve into mud.

O stuff we are of, have mercy. We love.

Filterless Pleasure

Black spots grew on the leaves, becoming some of light's voices.
Nourishment was darkened and sipped slowly up the veins.
The plant became itself
in company with illness.
It displayed itself in its way
but with additions and marks.

Neither rain, sun nor earth took notice.
Dew crept up from the ground.
Bumblebees sniffed and licked.
Animals moved past on special missions.

Stockboys smoked cigarettes and spat.
Trucks were unloaded. Dumpsters filled and stank.
Smells of dough and stale beer pushed the air.
Sweet clover sang its white and yellow notes
across knapweed and lace. Chinese lanterns
snuck over the fence. Sweet peas climbed it.
Bull thistle grew six feet high.

A human being walked past
and called the names and touched the leaves, held her nose
past dumpsters and air vents with bad breath.
She climbed up through the fence hole
to see dame's rockets and poppies.
The old man was watering his garden.

Trumpet Vine

While you swing at one end of the porch,
looking out through the screen, into the light,
all you can see of the vine at the other end
is its back, but you know that on its front
it's putting on a show: some slight-of-hand
with shiny leaves, a few card tricks
with orange flowers. If the trumpet vine
were death it could be that close to you,
right at the other end of your porch,
so near you could almost hear it breathing,
its face turned elsewhere for the moment.
You'd see no more than you see right now,
the back of an old coat, tattered with shadows.

Mussel Shells in Winter

Thrust through the frozen mud
they look like the shoulders of men
on some workaday errand,
wearing black overcoats with patches
through which white lining shows.

Where were they going that day,
hunched into the wind of water,
when by mistake they turned a corner
into the wrong street, not even
given so much as a last look back?

Kick one loose and toe it over,
and you'll see that the body is gone,
having been lifted away, perhaps
on snowy wings, leaving a shining,
immaculate brightness.

A Death

At the end, my uncle, whose kidneys had failed,
was covered with crystals of uric acid,
a salty white sand that sparkled on his skin.
We waited ten days for the tide to come in.

At First Light

At first light I left my sore body behind me.

Light as a curl of my mother's hair
I was lifted from worry
and without effort passed into childhood
through the smooth wooden tube
of a mourning dove's call.

I heard there the tambourine snap
of the screen door
into Bob McCullough's corner grocery.

In their rooms at the back,
his wife's sour-smelling Hoover
fretted and grumbled over the rugs.

Behind her, a pot of potatoes chuckled.

Then the dove called again, its low, sure whistle
like that of a departing train,
and I was borne back into the present,
an old man with sore teeth,
carrying candy, but only one piece,
pinched hard, a pastel Necco wafer, peach,
the last twenty flavors in that roll.

Satellite Dish

To all weathers I lift my gray face,
I raise my white fist, saluting the heavens.
I pray for those who sit alone tonight
in their flickering rooms: May they
receive a clear signal wherever they turn.
And may they be happy, at least for a time,
with the basic package.

Gib's Bar, Boise, Idaho, August 20, 1996

"Man, this has been great, hasn't this been great," Victor asks them. Joe laughs. "You were such a kid, such a baby, Joey, you really were, reading that poem about the hawk, you really were just—man, we are so old. Aren't we old?"

"You're not old," Mer says, "you can't say you're old."

"I'm 47. I'm almost 50. He's 45. You, you're young, but he's 45. That's not young."

"Yes, it is," Mer counters. Joe laughs. "What?"

"This is your chance, finally, Mer, to have someone think I'm old," he says and she smirks. "You think I look old enough to be her father, Vic."

"Yeah, sure, look at you. You look mean, your skin's rough. And look at her."

"Hey," Cheri says. "Want to play a game?"

Everyone stops and looks at her.

"Wow, you really purred that. A girl could learn from you," Mer says, making her father nervous.

"What game, baby?" Vic's fingers stroke her forearm.

"Confession, it's called."

"Uh-oh," Joe says. Vic gets a smile on his face like a fourteen-year-old, Mer thinks.

"Flip a quarter off your elbow and catch it in your palm. If you miss, take a shot. If you miss twice, take a shot and confess something—but it has to be a particular kind of confession."

"Flip a quarter off your elbow?" Joe stares at her. "This is a drinking game."

"The kind of confession is you have to confess something personal you were ashamed to know about yourself." Cheri's lips look shiny like a cherry automobile, Joe thinks, buzzed already.

"What kind of shots," Mer asks.

"Woh, wait a minute," Joe says.

"Any kind, whiskey, vodka, tequila," Cheri says.

"You're not saying anything, Vic," Joe says.

"Because I've got a hard-on."

"Jesus, Vic, shut up. Not in front of my daughter," Joe says, pronouncing the word like it rhymes with otter. Mer's amusement over Vic catches again on her father's speech. Cheri smiles at Mer, shakes her head.

"Okay, well, I could drink tequila but not whiskey," Mer says.

"No," Joe says.

"What do you mean, no?"

"No, no," he says, hands in the universal gesture of what's-the-problem?

"Well, whatever, drink what you want."

"That's not what I mean."

"Joe, she's 25," Vic says. "What were you drinking at 25?"

"She's with her old man," Cheri adds. "What can go wrong?"

"Let's not find out," he says and his daughter half-laughs.

"Okay, who goes first–well, we have to—" Mer starts, and Cheri calls out for a bottle of Jack and four shot glasses.

"You just got out of the hospital," Joe ducks toward Mer.

"Don't worry, Dad." It's a Western accent, she's hearing, shared by the indians, the Mexican Americans, the whites. She hears it in parts of Santa Fe and Espanola, and elsewhere around this bar, but never before in her father's voice.

"I can't be doing this," he shakes his head, and yet he is doing it. The bottle lands and they all kick in cash to pay for it. Joe shoves Mer's bills away, puts down double. Mer looks at him and laughs inside: this is weird, but it's good weird.

"I'll go first," Cheri says. "Then, we'll go around. Only on the second do you have to confess." Vic hands her a quarter.

"This is so fucked," Joe says.

"Hey," Vic objects, showing a row of spectacular teeth. "Not in front of your daughter!"

"Fuck you," Joe grins across the table.

"Gee, why's it fucked, Dad?" Mer asks, emphasizing the curse.

He glances at her, eyes glittery. Thin as she is right now, he thinks of her as a child, but he should know better.

"You take two shots it's easy to confess. You take more shots, it's easy to miss," he sighs.

"Ready?" Cheri puts the quarter on her forearm near the elbow and moves to catch the coin. She bats it across the room and it hits a chair. Everybody laughs.

"Beautiful, Cheri. I'll go get it." Vic staggers over, picks it up and walks back, handing it to Mer. He sits. Cheri pours a shot so it rises like a rain-filled river on the edge of the banks. Carefully, she lifts it. Everyone watches her grace. Her cherry upper lip dips in, and she knocks the honey colored liquor down.

"Hooo, chick. She knows how to drink," Vic says. This could be me, Joe thinks, wincing, a life's early turn taken back. Mer stands up.

"Up, that makes sense," Joe says, thinking he won't let her drink too much.

Mer puts the quarter on her left elbow, slips out from under it and catches it in her palm as it starts to fall. They all whoop as if at a sporting event, clap. She sits down, hands it to Joe. He looks at her for a moment, then stands up, gives it a shot, misses, gives the glass a shot and drinks. Vic misses, drinks. Cheri misses, drinks and thinks for a second.

"Okay, my confession, okay, what I found out—one thing I found out is how I really love doing what I do for a living, you know."

"What do you do for a living?" Mer hears her voice come forward in mock inquisitive, knowing it's probably seedy.

"Dance, I dance at parties, you know, for bachelors, business men. I know it bothers Vic," she rubs his arm, and his eyebrows raise. "But that's my confession. I'm ashamed that I love to dance naked over men's faces." She smiles, hands the quarter to the smooth-skin, goody two-shoes.

Such a cliche, Mer thinks, suspicious of it. She wants to shock me, she doesn't even know. Joe is shaking his head, looking at the women. It's like mixing oil paint with acrylic. Then, Mer gets up and does her coin trick again.

"I swear that looks like slow mo," Vic says.

Mer sits down, hands the coin to her father.

"Told you not to worry," she says, smug.

"Sassy. Bet she got it as a kid," Cheri says as Joe stands and tries again. The quarter ricochets under the table.

"Here, take a new one," he says and hands one from his pocket to Vic.

"You have to drink and confess, Dad."

"I know, I remember. No, she didn't," he says to Cheri.

"What," she frowns.

"Dad, confess," Mer says, mortified.

"What?" Cheri looks at Vic.

"She didn't get her ass kicked, Cheri," he says. "You just said—"

"Oh, oh, okay, okay, Jeez Louise," she says. She looked again at the girl, who averts her eyes. Spoiled brat.

"I'm ashamed to learn that I don't know anything," he says, and Mer smiles. There's silence.

"That's your confession?" Vic squints at him.

"Yeah, I think it's pretty big," Joe says, looking innocent and surprised.

"You fucker, that's no confession. You dishonor my woman. She just admitted something big," Vic says, though she was lying, or exaggerating.

"My suggestion is you just drink and confess, Vic. Forget the coin trick."

"Can you elaborate, poet?"

"What, no one said anything about interviewing the confessor."

Mer watches, amused, but with a little ice cube in the chest when Vic jolts.

"Honey, it's a game," Cheri says.

"Well, I'm going to flip the quarter anyway," he says, caught up in it, "and play fair." He misses, follows the rolling coin and stomps on it. "Dead!" He picks it up and walks back. "I confess that I'm ashamed that I like stealing cars. It feels like taking a girl's cherry, it makes me feel young," he says into Joe's eyes, knowing enough not to look at the kid's. He drinks the whiskey Cheri poured for him. Joe's expression stills as he thinks of Rick.

"Victor, you're such a bad boy," Cheri says. Mer rolls her eyes at the bad dialogue.

"We have to go," Joe says and Vic's expression shifts slightly sad.

"Wait," Cheri says, handing the quarter to Mer, who hasn't had anything stiff all evening. "I want to see you drink."

Mer takes the coin, stands up, puts it on her elbow. "It's so easy, you guys." The coin seems to wait for her in mid-air.

"You two are a pair of cons," Vic says, breaking the ice with a compliment. Joe smiles.

"It's your game. Set the rules better next time. Come on, let's all head out. You got me back." Joe pours a shot, drinks. "I confess I feel ashamed that I don't like to confess."

Vic laughs, stands up, helps Cheri up.

"I confess I said that to get a rise out of you. I feel so ashamed," Vic whines in mock sorrow, uncovering that snowfall of teeth.

"Take the bottle," Mer says. "We don't want it."

Cheri takes the neck in her manicured hand and Vic hovers over the lip with the cap, finally grabbing hold and screwing it on. Out in the parking lot, Joe feels like an idiot for drinking two shots of bourbon and two beers.

"Keys, Dad."

He digs in his pocket, tosses them.

"It was a pleasure to meet you both," Cheri says, shaking hands with them. Vic leans in and kisses the young girl's cheek. "Stay sweet," he says.

"Where'd you get that scar," Mer asks.

"Knife fight, age twelve."

"Twelve?" Dad's past keeps unraveling to a grainy B-movie, or an M.C. Escher print. Is it a gold fish or a bird of prey?

"He's always been a bad boy," Cheri says, wrapping her arm around the man.

"Yeah, yeah, a mischief-maker," Joe says. Vic laughs at the sarcasm, slaps Joe's back and starts away. "Good to see you, Man."

"Need help, Dad?"

"No, I don't." He walks to the driver's side.

"Hey," she says.

"Oh, yeah." He starts to walk around the hood of the Mazda.

"I confess," she says. He stops, looks back at her, with a smile until he sees her face.

"I had a miscarriage three years ago in a bathroom in the Providence public library and I hadn't even known I was pregnant. Rachel was there, but we didn't tell anyone. I didn't tell anyone. I didn't tell the guy, I didn't tell my father," she looks at him, waiting to see his expression. It's dark, but there is a phosphorescent bulb high above them. He walks over to her and she takes a step back.

"I'm ashamed I didn't know I was pregnant. I'm ashamed I didn't know I had appendicitis, I'm ashamed of hiding and run—"

"Stop that," he says, gently, and his arms hug her in that old way of being close, not fragile or suspicious. Me, I'm the suspicious one, Mer thinks.

"I'm ashamed—"

"I said, ssshhhh," he squeezes, so she relaxes into being hugged. "Rachel was with you?"

"Rachel was with me," she says, eyes watery. "And it hurt. It stole from me."

"I bet," he releases, looks at her, does what Rachel had, and takes her head in both hands. Again, she feels weary. "Mer, I'm so sorry. You should have told me. When was this?"

"July of '93. I was still in Providence teaching at the kids' camp. Covering bottles with yarn, making frogs out of clay," she says, with tears. His warm thumbs work like windshield wipers. He kisses the top of her head, lets go and grabs her shoulders.

"You're my kid, you'll always be my kid. I can't drink shots with you, but you can tell me anything," he says, and stops. It doesn't seem to matter how hard you try to shield someone if you're hiding, too. "You can be mad at me, but you can't run and hide, Mer. You can't do that to yourself, or me." He lets go of her arms. "You can't follow my rules for coping, you've got to make your own. That's not exactly fair, but I'm telling you to take a different route. You're standing on my map and I'm asking you to get off, I'm kicking you off. Include me, visit, but don't be me."

She sniffs away the tears tickling her nose, and frowns. Routes and roads and maps, driving, controlling the wheel. Poets and their metaphors. He watches her looking beyond his shoulder into the night. "Hmmm," she puffs.

"Can you drive," he asks.

"Yes, I can drive. I have my license, I'm over 18."

He smiles at her sarcasm, humor stiffening her soft pain. But, his mind is working.

"Eddy got you pregnant?"

"Yes, it was Eddy."

"Then he moved to Brazil."

"He didn't know. I didn't know," she said, but she hates the sound of herself defending him.

"You had a sexual relationship with him. Do you think if the two of you knew, he would have forfeited Brazil?"

"Oh, no," she says. "Never."

"Yeah," he says, insulted.

"And that's okay, though, because he's better at a distance. You know, he gives the impression that he loves me, that he's capable of intimacy. His letters are intimate, they chafe against the inside of the envelopes," she smiles at her joke. The early days were no different, though, when he drew her to the dance floor and gradually shifted into a group of dancers next to them and was swallowed whole. She would not see him, not for an hour, and then he'd catch up, all excited, oblivious. "Distance is better at a distance, instead of in the room with me, I realize. And this is the difference. I know how he fooled me—not on purpose, but certainly, still selfishly—and I know how I let him." She shrugs her shoulders. Joe's heart aches.

"I'm not convinced you're safe," he says.

"I'm blowing him off, if that's what you mean."

"No, I mean that I'm not sure I'll ever feel unafraid for you. I'll have confidence in you, I do, but I won't stop worrying."

"Well, must you?" She tried to lighten it, but you can't lighten sludge. "What if I had said to you right out of college that I was pregnant?"

"I'd say the apple does not fall far from the tree."

"What did you forfeit?"

"Nothing," he says.

"Really, Dad, what did you forfeit?"

"Nothing. School, but I knew what I wanted to do and that didn't require a degree. I had a newspaper job. I did exchange one sense of myself for another, but it took me years to see that. I'd never seen myself with any tangible future, even though I just said I liked to write. Being married because of you could've backfired, but it didn't, it made me go for it, get aggressive. I'd never thought I'd be a father, as a kid I wasn't thinking I'd get married. I was bored when I was fifteen, and I liked Elsie Fish, and if things hadn't happened the way they did, stealing the car, etcetera, maybe I'd have married her for the same reason, or maybe I would have bolted. She was sweet and earnest, funny, and I don't remember who I was. I'd be Victor, now, or my brother, ex-cons with small lives, girlfriends who make other men happy." He still doesn't want to wake her up to it, doesn't want her to see him, clearly.

"Tonight, I heard your voice change. I heard you say café, like Nescafe, and flatten your tones. I heard you sound like them."

"Really, I didn't notice."

"You had an accent and got rid of it?"

"Yes."

"Consciously?"

"Oh, yeah."

"Why?"

"I didn't want to be from people who didn't care about me. I didn't want to hear them whenever I spoke," he says.

"Wow, that's terrible. We shouldn't be taking this detour."

"No, we should. This time I've got you to show for my life, and nothing to prove. There is nothing to prove, or defend. But I can give you to them and them to you."

"Question is, are we disappointing?" She sees him frown, shake his head. "I'd have a toddler by now if—"

"Stop that, damn it. They come when they should."

"I guess I wasn't ready."

"No one is ready, Mer. But, really, it isn't just you accepting the new life. It's the new life accepting the journey. They come when they're ready."

She smiles, softly. His spirituality is a funny thing, his sense of the journey. Am I following his road map? Didn't I navigate in the front seat of the car as a kid, Rand McNally open on my lap? She lights up. "Oh, hey, let me help you roll up this hefty map," she jumps away from him.

"You are sassy," he says, walking over to the passenger side of the car, smiling.

She unlocks the door. "Why did you bother getting offended by Cheri?"

"I wasn't offended. I don't like that attitude, that's all." Kids getting beat for every opinion, he thinks.

Inside, they get comfortable in their seats. It's always a balance between having enough legroom and feeling secure to drive, not so distant from the road, not so relaxed, Mer thinks. Joe stares ahead of him, slowly scowling.

"Tell me you went to the hospital," he says, looking at his hands.

"What?" Mer stops with the seatbelt and looks out the windshield, not at him. "No, I didn't. I didn't tell anyone."

"You had a miscarriage in a public bathroom and you didn't go to the hospital?"

"No," she whimpers, feeling the weight of it coming back.

"Rachel didn't take you," he can't help his voice.

"No, she took me home, she stayed with me."

"You could have hemorrhaged."

"Dad, it was very painful and then it was over," she says, turning to him and looking keenly at his eyes. "Over." Like fluttering wings escaping or the idea of a sparrow falling out of her.

"You flushed the toilet," he asks, and she drops the keys and opens the door, getting out of the car.

"Mer, don't get out," he says, but she shuts the door and walks away from the car, looking around. He gets out, and sees her running back to the bar. He follows her and when he gets inside, sees her head into the bathroom. "Mer," he says, sadly. He sits at a table for a couple minutes and waits. In the bathroom, Mer looks at herself in the mirror and sees pale, unkind and lonely. Joe remembers Mer's keys and goes out to the parking lot.

"No, no, no," he runs into the dark center of the lot and looks around, but it's gone. He walks back into the bar and asks the bartender for a phone to make a local. He gets a cordless and punches in some numbers. In the bathroom, Mer splashes cold water on her face to make the tears stop lurking in her bones beneath her eyes. To freeze them there. Then, she goes into the stall, but backs out.

"Miss, you okay," a voice asks behind her and she turns to see a woman in her thirties with an open lipstick tube.

"Basically," she says. "Thanks."

"That guy out there your old man?"

"Yeah, in one sense. He's my father."

"Right, that's what I thought."

"That's refreshing. All my life people said he looked too young to be my father, as if they were accusing me of taking something away from him—"

"Them, maybe."

"Or them, probably. But this trip I wonder if people might think I was his chippy," she says. The woman laughed.

"He moves like a father," she says, capping her lipstick.

"Really?"

"There's a look some of them have, the ones who like their kids, and gestures, a gaze."

"You're observant."

"Well, I work with families. Have a good night," she smiles. Mer catches the rhythm of that, the down sweep of families, the optimism of good night.

"You, too," she says. She stands at the sinks and takes deep breaths before walking back out. She sees her father at a table with two mugs of coffee, so she goes and sits.

"Somebody stole your car," he says.

"No," she stands up.

"Since you left the keys on the seat of your sports car, it was like an invitation."

Mer looks at him. "I left you in the car. You could have grabbed them."

"Have a cup of coffee."

"Did you call the police?"

"I called Vic. He's coming to pick us up. He'll find out where it is."

She sits down. His voice is back to normal or, what she's familiar with. "Well, I guess that settles the issue about the car," she says as she pours milk into the mug to the color of bourbon. "It's just that my license is in the glove compartment."

"Not on you?"

"No, I like to travel light. And I'm old enough to drink, I don't usually get carded."

"Great," he says, annoyed. "I've every right to be worried about you."

"I know, but it's not okay to make me feel bad," she says, lowering her voice. "Yes, we flushed my fetus, and I didn't go to the hospital because I couldn't bear the fact that I didn't know I'd been pregnant. I was embarrassed in front of Rachel, and horrified that I had been partying at the end of school. I was hurt that I hurt another human being and pushed it out of me. I didn't think that I was physically in danger. I was dangerous."

Joe reaches out and holds her wrist, looks at those evergreen eyes, pale skin.

"Isn't Rachel from a family of doctors?"

"Yes, so she knew what to do with me in the face of my refusal to move. She stayed while I lay on my bed at home." Mer takes a deep breath. "I can see that I should have gone. But, I didn't."

"Right, but I'm getting this news late, Mer, and it's big news. It's a terrible thing to go through almost all alone, and remember, I care about you. It seems like this is the reason you've been withdrawing, and I don't know where I was, or how I didn't notice. I haven't seen you much. It's not really true that you let your kid go when she grows up, you just lose your rights. I care just as much. I was not trying to shame you by asking if you flushed it. I just want to know how this could have happened the way it did, and how you could be alone, but for your dog, when your appendix burst, headed across fifteen states to go see the guy who left you. 72 hours after that thing burst that you hit the hospital. You just kept driving, staying in murder motels, bearing the pain, Goddammit, sweet dove. Poison all over, trying to kill you." His face is contorting with his own pain and he feels it all over. He holds onto her wrist in case she wants to run. "Do you know what this does to me? Can you imagine me spreading my hand," and he lets go to use his left hand to fan his fingers, "and placing it over your sleeping infant body, feeling it vibrate lightly as a living person, heart thumpety thump right into my index finger. Maybe you don't want to hear this now, when you lost a beginning, but maybe that means you can know how I cannot lose you in any way. Already, you've had two wretched things happen, and that's enough."

"I'm 25, and I don't know what I'm doing, and I feel so stupid, especially in front of you, and in memory of Mom, when you two had me and jobs and a house when you were 25," she says, hyper. That's a skewed picture she's painting him and not the one he remembers. "I keep thinking that just around the corner is my better life, my proof to you that I'm worth all the trouble."

"Woh, what?

"All that you sacrificed to raise me after she died, all you gave up, and—"

"Hey, hey," Vic strolls over and sits down. "Sorry about your car, girly."

"Oh, well, it was a stupid mistake," she sits up, pretends she's okay. Joe is angry, but he tries to hide it. He looks at Vic.

"It'll be okay, we'll catch them, get your car back. It might be like a model kit, but," he tosses his hand back.

"Are you sure, Vic? I'm sorry." Mer asks.

"Sure I'm sure, you don't know me, and you don't want to, and he doesn't want you to, either, but I can summarize for you. We'll get your car," he stares at her. "Don't be glum."

"Her license is in the glove compartment, any chance we'll get that?" Joe asks, and Mer feels like she's fifteen and in trouble.

"If not, we'll make a new one," he laughs. "Oh, hey, hey, sip your coffee and come along with me."

"Are you able to drive," Mer asks, taking a bitter swallow.

"Do you have a choice?"

"Yes, I have a choice," she says, leaning back in her chair. Joe smiles.

"Can you drive stick, girly?"

"Of course," she says.

"Just don't leave them on the seat," Vic says, passing her his keys.

5 *Poems*

For Harvey Shapiro

5 PM. Often
rain, thunder. More CO_2?
"No," your view, "God's wrath."

' ' '

Summer's starved-bluefish,
sea-churn silver. Winter's birth-
day, cake-sugar dust.

For M. Ziesk

Ounce pain, till temples'
balanced pressure. Jarred frames show:
past, past; rebalance.

For C.

Film-star daughter. Same
face bones; black hair, not white-blonde.
How dark a sun chars.

For Michael Heller

Krishna's dolls: child to
bones. Beast axing a man-faced
cow: *thoughts' death—and death:*

thought champagne kills. Glass at
lips—though nova out Earth.

For David Ignatow

Some cut boards, breathe saw-
dust; gut fish. Some chart stars. So
far—who catches them?

High School

Enamored of Euclid's circles and squares.

Van Doren's *World Poetry*:
orated to brainy, Episcopal Judith.

Or rhymed hot "God" and "love,"
useless as seduction.

Slip straps under a sheer blouse.
Screwing the college boyfriend.

(Did I care? Knowledge was power?)

Though in English Miss H. alleged:
I "stole" Bradbury, Salinger.

(Was I her techie? not a wordsmith?)

Alone, I intoned my people's long lines,
precursing Whitman.

Read Bell's mathematical *Lives*.

Daydreamed torrid lips of Judith,
unkissed before pure number.

Cadenza for the Works of Nick Cave and Euridice

And like a pollen burst we languidly rise, fall,
right-left, northeast and southwest across intimate globes.

Squeeze my hand so I have the energy to hike across. Give me
air time and a radio interview so I can disseminate the plane of
        stars
to ears. Pull the plugs.

Fifty white-bellied gulls on a yellow crane are the closest thing
to the rule of this land I can hear. I always know they are there
and I don't believe in the existence of angels—
looking at you I wonder if it is true,

just like the memory of hot air at the arc of your little
ear. The only sense we have is touch and wave:
we make it, slowly, pushing
our ball up any hill.
We make it with fat hearts beating under a cage of bone—
a needle of light threads the course of a river,
current into the brown of your eye,
branch and bough into the teacups of your ears
filled with melody-nectar quivered by a lute—
touch and wave
good
bye.

> *I remember a girl so very well,*
> *the carnival drums all mad in the air,*
> a horse with violet hair
> whinnies and whinnies, opening
> up and if she could she'd ride right inside its belly
> off toward.
>   Life tunes its trembling string.

My tongue is a sphere in disguise and knows how
    to roll.
My tongue is a black swift that knows when to dart with the flock
    but resists.
My tongue is a lute and tears up oaks, melts the hearts of tiger-
    lilies.

When I crawl into your arms, Euridice,
Everything comes tumbling down
The verve of speech especially.

I resorted to pajama stories and lasted
    a while little,
I resorted to the clichés of Love and the Thracians
    pulled me to shreds.

I'll take a handful of weeping and sorrow-parting
(The birds are there, if you stare.)
I'll take a walk in the park
and name you Darling.

I am confused about the sum of your olive skin,
of three evenings on a break-wall watching waves rupture all
for calm,
and two at the keyboard.

The snowplows are out and I beat them for taking you away,
you the snow and the passenger.

The world fell past, parking in a dusted snow
field and the crescendo of light reflecting off
a duck's wings sparking against river kissed mist
as I ran and spun in place behind the steering wheel,
bending over to you like a really big fucking feather
weighted with fifteen feet of pure white snow, my quill
at the nape of your neck scribbling everything
that a man has to say, and trying to sing

the stars into place silently to spotlight our love
letter through the windshield, how it was torn and puzzled
back together and we were pressed to the glass projecting
our cinematography to deer and gnomes whose hats
were taunting tongues, jealous of our fit and film-longing.

You are the skin of a holiday, the lime of a star
hung out on the thick and crowded tree of night.

If my song is drawn out completely I am dead;
so I hold my breath
so I don't lose the plot,
so I don't grow soft.

We fucked up the sun and then fucked it down again:
I delay the bite with my own, and you
foretell the future with yours.
I massage the walls of your temples to tempt you
to sleep and dream,

Euridice slips her tongue

Someone says *what are you screaming for?*
The plot the plot!

Farewell, she said, a last Farewell

Wake up my lover,
my lover wake up.

Immortal Sofa

"I sing the sofa"
– William Cowper

When I see sofas hauled from student dumps,
and set out on the curb in heavy showers,
I know it's spring. Time to clear out of here,
start life again with nothing but a suitcase.
But here's my house. Yes, I admit I'm staying.
My sofa won't be going out the door.
Instead I join the cat asleep on the afghan,
warm my hands on a hot mug of tea,
and remember my mother-in-law's rowhouse
in Baltimore, crammed with quilted armchairs,
glass ash trays deep as bird baths, cattails
dried to mauve, stuck in a Chinese vase.
No wonder I vowed never to own anything,
no Turkish carpets, lamps, or cabinets,
especially not a long, three-cushion sofa
covered in protective dull green serge,
antimacassars of yellow lace on the armrests..
Ah, but my mother-in-law secretly longed
to buy an off-white love-seat at Sears
and here was her chance to finally give away
a ten-year-old sofa in perfect condition.
Too poor to refuse, my husband and I
U-hauled the sofa down to Virginia,
where it mildewed in storage for a year
until we found a larger place to live.
We used to lounge, legs tangled, after work,
drinking gimlets, talking about dream cities.
Slowly the sofa rose up, carrying us
out the sliding doors of our apartment.
Far below we'd see the twinkling lights

of Richmond, some barges on the James,
mowed sweeps of battlefields and cemeteries
getting smaller as the sofa flew higher,
rushing along the highways of air, headed
for the Andes, or the jungles of Brazil.
And sometimes we'd be set down, gently,
on the outskirts of Cuzco or Asuncion
dazed by herds of llama, or red cattle
that parted to sweep past our magic sofa.
Or we might float over a foaming waterfall
inches above a rainbow, giddy and dizzy,
scared but safe on our familiar cushions.
But when we finally moved to California,
owners of beds, tables, desks, and chairs
and boxes of things of all sorts and sizes,
we took the dirty cover off the sofa,
discovering chartreuse satin brocade.
Yet though it looked shiny and brand-new
against the ugly black and white swirled carpet
of our rented bungalow in Hell,
the sofa couldn't fly under the weight
of two hearts heavy as the redwood
sliced and polished into our coffee table.
We'd stumble home from work with umbrellas,
turn the cold knob on the gas space-heater,
then head to bed. So maybe we were dreaming
suddenly to find new jobs under palms
in Arizona, my mother-in-law
arriving to sit on her old sofa, shrunken
as if she'd stepped from a fun-house mirror,
remarking on the good quality of the fabric.
Then she was dead, outlived by the sofa
which moved into this house in Indiana,
barely fitting through the angled hallway.
Clawed by cats, flea-sprayed, recovered
in blue velvet, the sofa sags and dips
from indentations of spines and buttocks
of all the people who've ever sat here

to talk, or read, or put their feet up,
one warm impression after another
loosening, crushing, squashing, flattening.
Once we tried to buy a stylish sofa
but though the workmen unhinged the door
and laid it flat in the snow, they couldn't
wedge the new one inside, and took it back,
leaving this one safe for years to come.
How many books have I read sitting here?
How many times have I returned from trips
glad to fling myself on these battered cushions?
If ever I get to wander the roomy clouds
of Heaven, my golden cup of nectar
brimming over, I'll look for my sofa.
I think I'll find it far from the incense
and the loud hosannas, a quiet spot
for those who'd rather doze a bit, and dream,
than sing loudly with the choirs of angels.

Under the Sign of Fire

Obsessive, I grieve the end
Of each day, each book I read,
Each bowl of morning yogurt rinsed clean.
I hate the word over
Whether it's a minute or a season.

A man once called me *melodramatic*.
I don't think so. So what if I broke
Like porcelain over that table,
The flame of the candle between him and me,
Making a wave in a glass dome, his face
Stripped of all its defenses, like a child's
Rising from sleep when I asked him
What he expected of me. Struck
Dumb, he couldn't answer.

I am red-haired; I was born
Under the sign of fire
And I burn with such intensity
No one will touch me.
My life is a torch
That consumes everything I want or love.

At four o'clock, the courthouse
Tower sounds as many bells.
The little evening birds begin
Their sad, sweet repetitions,
Like a girl practicing piano.
The hammer strikes the strings
And the elemental air,
Which also feeds the fire,
Carries the endless noises of the world,
And fuels the flaming sorrow in me.

Family of Hard Workers

I would like to forget
That I come from a family of hard workers:
Grandfather of axe-handles carved
For the Georgia railroad, Grandmother
Of thirteen children flinging feed for the chickens
From a fifty-pound bag, forgive me,
I forget you. And if my father glorifies
What is, in actuality, a certain lack of choices
On the part of his relatives
Who rose at the cock's crow
And made a day so similar to the one before it
That if someone asked what they'd done that day,
They would stand with their hands in their pockets
Then give you their one answer:
I whittled an axe handle. I fed the chickens.
Then, forgive me, for not doing that, too.

Once, I kept a carved statue of a horse
On my window sill,
The right, front leg crooked like a little finger
Which made the horse seem always in motion.
It's all I remember about the horse,
The arched leg ready to step
Into the green pastures of my imagination
And thrum with its hooves,
Churning up grass, unhaltered, unsaddled,
Its huge head rivening the wind.
Better if my father had said:
You come from a family
Where beauty matters.
Look at the horse, now,
Running for joy.

When He Prunes the Roses

From the upstairs window
I watch him unload the long-handled shovel
And the rusty bucket from the old truck's bed,
Listen to him unlock the white gate
And begin to clip:
His scissors are like a latch
Opening and closing under me.

I can tell, when he moves,
Just where he is
In what part of the garden:
Louder, now, in the red Jessica,
Fainter in the Old Blush from China.
What would bring a man
Who was once a logger
To tend old roses?
He bends over the bed
Taking in the intimacy of scent
The white Albas release.
Clearly, he is lingering,
Taking what he can from the canes
Until the shade shifts
And he flickers in and out of light
Hauling away the cut stalks.

You should see him, how he touches
The petals, like panties in his hands—
Pink and white and red
As he loosens them,
Dropping them into his blue bandana,
Then folding it over.

A Different Language

All I want is a soda
From the Chinese take-out booth
In the mall. The woman
Behind the register doesn't speak English
But points to the Coke sign
Above her, a flashing neon flag
The one word we both know.

The woman holds up six fingers
And I count two quarters
And a dime from my fuchsia, leather
Coin pouch, which seems like a scream
Lying there, under the dignified gaze
Of the waitress,
Her precise hands pushing the buttons
And the register bell ringing
Like a signal from the kitchen
That the shrimp is ready.

She slides a soda across the counter
And smiles until, somehow, I feel we're friends
As I sit outside the mall
On a bench and sip my Coke
Through a red and white striped straw
Like a kid sucking a candy cane.
Pigeons peck around my feet
For bread, but I don't have any.
We all are willing to make trades:
People bow to each other,
And my dog, at home,
Knows to lift one paw for a biscuit.

Karen Whalley

French Rose

It is the day after Thanksgiving,
The year terrorists
Toppled two buildings in the name of religion
And gave Americans the gift
Of humility and took from them a certain innocence.
It is the year
In which I fell out of love—
Or he fell out of love with me,
Which is really the long angel's fall
From grace, from the heaven
A good feeling makes between two people,
And I learned redemption
Is passing up the opportunity
To stay in pain.

I am watching the apple tree
Drop precisely one apple per day,
As if it has mastered the beautiful art
Of giving up, and in that nudity
It is free of red ornaments
Like the vulnerable face
Of a woman without lipstick
Who has made her peace
With the pretenses of the world.

I am poor, and single.
I am poor and married
To the idea of happiness, the same way *sky*
Is the only word for *blue*.
Because it's my birthday,
I bathed this morning
In the French rose soap
My sister bought for me
At a ritzy store in an upscale mall
Proving there is a world

Where people care about the way things smell
And the delicate, carved *M*
In the top of the bar
Like a secret initial to some exclusive club
So that a woman like myself
Might rise one morning
From the sweet and steamy bath
Into cold November air,
Slick and pink from the hot water
Ready to begin again with a faith
Odd as a terrorist's, thinking, *This is how you live, this*
Is what you do.

American Incident

Knowing which way to bend
does little to recommend a way of being
in an unbearable world.
At least that's what I heard
yesterday while waiting for the squirrel
to descend from its tree:

wisdom will not fall on you
like a promiscuous acorn, escort
you to the dance with your seventh-grade crush
while you wait it out in the shadows
wishing for an acceptable form of self-pity.

' ' '

To truck with the saint
you think has occupied your head
is to call your soul into question
as the thick mixture it is.

Why deliver such hardship
upon yourself, and in this heat?

Judging by the neighbors' dirty looks
the muffler needs replacing.

My credit card was snatched,
cut in half when I tried to buy
your birthday present at the feed store.

' ' '

A borrowed sweater can be the cause

of great sorrow to its owner
when the first thread to separate
continues in its course
enlisting others with it so fast
the borrower hurries to return what
in the end will mean the end
of what connects the owner and
the innocent one blamed for
what's unraveled onto the floor.

' ' '

I can't say what's in order except that
I feel at ease with it.
I welcome it
gnarled on the inside
as it might be.
Immeasure ably provides,
ripped right through.
Take care,
that's not what I wanted.
Yours is dying to be
Yours truly.

' ' '

If you feel you have no culture,
say "I have no culture" to everyone you meet.

This will generate conversation
where the possibility did not exist before.

' ' '

You are not alone in your fear
of dogs, their sniffing and snapping,
their beautifully pointless bodies.
Nothing will please you without pain.

When you broke something deep inside
you pretended to be on the mend,
dashed your head against the desk instead.
The drama of it makes one swoon.

' ' '

The stupidity of youth asserts itself
there, where you hear tires assault the curve,
bottles drop beside cans of beer,
the whisper, here, of how to forget the day
we didn't spend together we never will have spent
together, the substance of rebuke.

' ' '

Quite a tug of war flagrant as migrating trash,
severagation at work on the town, it works
up to a point: everyone steers clear
of everyone else, speaks only when spoken.

' ' '

Some wicked thought, when it fails to disrupt
the day with its sordidness, disrupts through its failure:

a second-order moral quandary,
the concern of not being sufficiently concerned.

' ' '

Our backers have been generous
to a point; beyond this point
they dip into churlishness.

To dip into churlishness invites
unhealthy comparisons
which in turn invite envy.

One must stop this chain before
it brings you to your mother
-in-law's doorstep weeping.

' ' '

A beer can on the front lawn,
when empty, is just a can—
not a grail, not an extinguisher.

' ' '

A way to close, perhaps, a last move,
to leave oneself wide open to attack
("his poems make a noise that threatens
to never quit") but one of these keys
is sticking and the trick becomes how
to avoid words with the offending letter:
this lends a fixed form to the poem,
a form distinct to this machine
and time, as it must be fixed, and soon.

' ' '

The man pissing
against the bridge's railing mis-
takes the river for a river,
walks away content.

Hands off

He's just a red pulse, a six-foot hump,
a dogmeat heart in a surgeon's grip.
Even the thick, pea-green tufts of rug
parted when she up and crossed the sea
of *good-bye honey*, the tight screen door
snapping its one snare note
like a fast hand on his ass. For years,
she was almost rain in the cactus heat,
until one night as she slept he stared
like a dry gun at the naked curl
of her back, all lit up by a static moon.
Hours of study, his aching arm, his hand
out over her damp skin, the inches
between them firing like nerves.
He felt bigger than thick sky, tough
as root. His hurt bulged like rocks,
like orders not to touch, and one month
later she left real calm, like she'd
had a reservation since their first night.
No kiss. Just the sharp door and
her tight jeans hissing to the car,
leaving him this ugly hulk all puffed up
and full of suicide so manly, he imagines
knives. Or better: the propane tank
out back, a grievous suck, a longest
last breath to the deep guts. But when
he closes his eyes into this tough-assed
pretty boy picture, he likes the new look,
his soul flexed, shining like a muscle
beneath the skin. Now a surge,
what he's got coming to him real good.
He could have stuck his big arm out there,
could have pulled her back to him quick,

her crotch stuffed against his like a deal.
But the good deep hurt held him back,
the low searing, hot and pressed up
against his skin from the inside, a living
thing, a lung throbbing, a best friend.
He can feel it in his spine like always,
coming up so slow he could snap,
the clock counting two, three
in the holy ay em. Hurt like this,
he'll live with her sweet ass gone.
He'll never begin to touch himself.

The Crossing

When had he disappeared? Fifty,
divorced, slathering through tomes
on super-strings and hyperspace,
peering into the interstices
of mathematical white noise, hoping
to disprove Nietzsche and all the French.
She's gone. A trail of atomized scents
blurred like hidden galaxies in the dust
of his telescope. Long ago, in the days
of the stoned subjunctive, the roach clip
tipped with the last gleam of lit weed,
the seamless rock fugue of Mark-Almond
bearing an ideal into the smoke-carved airs,
he imagined skin like pearl muslin, hair
like incense, the music slow as dusk
on acid. He imagined the anatomy
of his transcendence. It didn't matter
he didn't know her yet. If ever
she ascended the stairs, if ever
in the dim twilight her breasts shone
above him, if she purled on the low
mattress as if it were a raft on an ocean
of sweet cream, if just then the music
rose open as she did, hell, then
the crossing might begin. Who knew
in the patchouli dark the altitude
of enlightenment? No one. He knew
it was there, mystic, reachable,
an urgent proton slowing
to the synaptic edge of each nerve.
Then the change. A sexual physics
to deliver a high so bodiless
he'd become pure brain power.
By then, he'd already given up
on his Catholic ascendancies, the neat

trellis of sacramental steps to a sure-thing
afterlife of misty bliss. Too fixed,
too anthropomorphic to believe.
Now it's all a lost bet. The spectra
of particle waves and his own
predictable future. Nothing passes
for bedrock faith. His ex-wife merely
a woman in this dull life. A dream
swirls on the dark ceiling above him.
Dust motes. Galaxial incense. Erotic twirl.

DEMONSTRATION

CROWDED SOUR HUMAN BODIES LINED
FOR AND AGAINST ANY ONE THING
FEET WHAPPING CEMENT CHANTS CURSES
POLICE BATONS HORIZONTAL PUSHING
BACK AMERICA WHERE NOTHING HAPPENS
ON THE STREETS MAKES A DIFFERENCE.

LET'S PAUSE TO DIGEST THAT LAST
GENERALIZATION WHILE PROTESTORS GLEEFULLY
AND SYMBOLICALLY FILL POLICE VANS.

IS IT BETTER TO CYNICALLY VIEW
THE SCENE FROM THIS SAFE DISTANCE?
OR LIKE EVERY SLEEPER BENEATH THE
OVERPASS INCORPORATE IT INTO FITFUL
DREAMS?

LET'S TRY THIS: COMFORTABLE SHOES ARE
NECESSARY TO DO BUSINESS IN THIS COUNTRY.
I DO NOT KNOW WHAT THE SLEEPERS DREAM
AND WHO IS INFECTED WITH WHAT BLUE DRUG
BUT I PROMISE THE FOUNDING FATHERS DO
NOT COME INTO PLAY. COMFORT IN THE STINK
HOWEVER TEMPORARY. HOWEVER.

WALL OF THE HUMAN HEART

EACH BRICK SLEEPS IN ITS OWN BED
WE ARE UNFORGIVEN THE SPITEFUL
MISSPELLINGS OF OUR OWN NAMES MORTAR
ERODES YOU. ME

after rain
beaded water glistens
on the black wire

EACH WINDOW BOXED
INTO NINE PANELS
VISION CUT BOXCARS

Missing hyphens
merge passively into the hesitation

of dashes

SACRAMENTS from a menu
DREAMS interrupted

the crash of the unmistakable

broken glass, a cut

the hissing crackle
of an electric snake

GRIT OF MORTAR
DUST OF PRAYER

THE WALLS COME A TUMBLING
WALLS COME A TUMBLING
DOWN

rosary of water disrupted
by a sparrow

a catalog of grudges
color coded

sledge HAMMER smash BRICK

future already evaporating

the fuse of everything we don't know

LOVE WEED

TWELVE CLEAN BRICKS ONE GREEN HALO
    BLOOMING IN CRACKED STEP
ONE PRIEST TWELVE UNSHAVEN CHEEKS
    ONE BLUE HAND BARED AND SCRAPED
JOURNEY OF KNUCKLES AND DREAM
    LEAKING WEARING AWAY THE ONE SPOT
WHERE THE KNOT WAS UNTIED BRIEFLY.

Cover Letters

Dear Sir or Madam,

I am a depressive, and have always been one. My greatest desire is to lie down, curl into a little ball, and never wake up again. That notwithstanding, I think I would make an effective and helpful addition to your marketing department.

Dear Sir or Madam,

How does something go from being a product to being a commodity? I did my graduate thesis on this subject, so I feel uniquely qualified to bring an analytical awareness to marketing Snapple beverages. For example: Does a bottle of juice *qua* juice constitute a construction of desire or a mere supply-and-demand image of same? I explored this question in my thesis, employing considerations of gender, race, colonialism and Marxist theory. I therefore feel I have worthwhile contributions to make to a department of copywriters for Snapple.

Dear Sir or Madam,

Recovering crack addicts have important insights into consumer patterns. When it comes to marketing a sugar-based drink like Snapple, I have the inside track. Former colleagues I shared work detail with in venues like the laundry, the bathrooms, and metal shop have all given me insight into who needs what kind of stimulant when. It's a simple step from there to knowing how to remind someone of a need for their stimulant. I'm not just talking through my hat. I run a successful service that supplies people with stimulants they need and enjoy, and are willing to pay way more than market value for. I have a good reputation on my block, and can provide references easily, though addresses and phone numbers might be more of a problem. As for a possible drug test, all I can say is: Do you want profits to go up or not?

Dear Sir or Madam,

I don't have any of the qualifications listed in your ad. But why not take a chance on someone who doesn't have any marketing experience per se, but is hyper-smart and could learn the business within a few hours? I have an IQ of 180, score out of the stratosphere on every standardized test, and am generally way smarter than the people I work with. You might be wondering why I don't have more work experience. It's because I get bored working with stupid dipshits! When Mr. I'm-in-Charge-of-You can't figure out a simple computer program for mailing labels, I'm like laughing practically in his face! But at Snapple, I'm sure people wouldn't be that dumb.

Dear Sir or Madam,

Do you like flowers and tropical fruit? Do you like steam rooms and oil rubs? I want to suck you and fuck you upside down and sideways, I want to screw you senseless till the idea of marketing Snapple is a pinpoint in your brain, but we do it anyway, later.

Dear Sir or Madam,

It's me again. I still want to fuck you senseless, pressing my sex against you till you are ready to explode. I want to rub thin vibrating finger-condoms all over your body, then sluice you with lubricant and totally explore every inch of your flesh. I'm serious, I'm really getting into this. I don't care if I get the job or not.

Dear Sir and Madam,

The long gaps in my work history can be explained by a mood disorder that has resulted in periods of hospitalization. But this does not mean I am not suited to working as a copywriter for Snapple. When you're institutionalized, you have a lot of time on your hands. When you happen to be institutionalized in a capitalist country, what do you think about? Selling fruit beverages! Dynamic marketing schemes can be concocted within the slack, lagging time frames of the average day in a psych ward. And plenty of creative boosts can be found from the exciting pharmaceutical treatment I underwent while in the hospital. So the ideas I have to contribute are, I think, pretty valuable compared to more "normal" ideas.

Dear Sir or Madam,

Once again, it's me. Have you thought about the lubricant? Have you thought about my hands probing every notch and crevice of your—oh never mind. I have lots of people I can have sex with. I just thought you might be into this. But your lack of response is seriously chilling my jones for you.

Owl—Cyva

I.

I translated its wings, the black sails
  of exacting eyes,

feathers snow-speckled, talons hooking
  a long oak branch.

I translated my opened hands into light
  against a bare March sky,

the heat of splintered wood. I breathed in,
  exhaled a gray feather

fallen across a winter meadow
  in which a house would be built,

its family asleep behind a closed door.
  I breathed in *hare*,

exhaled an exclamation mark
  before turning the page.

II.

And in a first dream of spring floods,
  the frogs cry-croak, roused by water,

and through the sound of rain, more rain –
  a house mushrooming,

its family asleep under the first blank page,

winter following rain,

mice carrying grain. Inside, a warming stove,
night floating like a feather

becoming *moon* outside my window,
before the window opened into *voice*

and *voice* into a fox's throat, and *I*
a feather that could not be named.

III.

Eyes of a woman drowned in her tub, Solomea,
in Kiev, on the eve of the new millennium,

at the mouth of a river I know only by *Desna*—
bones, hair, the disk of her face.

I call her *Cyva*, a nocturnal bird, heard her song.
I raise the oars of a small canoe

and see a man, a friend, Ed, look up
through water, a notebook still

in his hand, his eyes moving, as if reading –
the shadow of a willow

that buries him. I took to my lips
the language of my mother, father,

sister, the language of birds
in a tree at night outside of a room

where I read waiting for the river,
for words that would hunt by night.

Who Forgives Whom

Who forgives whom in the moment
of slow ascending, lifted from the body

badly bruised for a sigh,
in that moment less than sacred

when there are no bidders
no God disguised in bright children's clothes,

singing, pushing a stroller down the sidewalk
into a crack.

How can I lend you that same dark dress
the one in which my mother was married

during the war, a stolen bouquet
of flowers in her hands, inside

an unnamed stone chapel, her lime
green rosary, weightless crucifix,

too easily broken to hold Christ.
All morning, the sky lets go

of what it no longer harbors:
long needles of lightning

the blue disappearing,
Ask if blood still binds,

how you can look so white lying there,
my hair, longer than I remember it,

fanned across my bed,
Whose eyes enter ours?

Someone else's notion of heaven,
each breath like a bird leaving our bodies

never claiming to know holy
or cry out for it.

Fancy Dinosaur

I was ironing my fancy soul when the phone rang. It was God. He said, *I'm not dead, and I'm calling those who still iron their fancy souls to give me praise*. This had become one of those moments when you want to say just the right thing and have no regrets later on. While I was paused, formulating the perfect sentence, I smelled smoke. I looked in the kitchen and saw I'd left the iron on my fancy soul. I dropped the phone and ran to the ironing board. I picked up the iron, and seared into my fancy soul was a black mark of regret, just the thing I'd hoped to avoid. When I picked up the phone again, there was a dial tone, a swarm of a million angry wasps, the sound of eternity without God.

Narcissus

All the best tales of survival still end with death. We carry our crosses etched in the cool stones that mark our graves. And that laughter that won't stop is not of this world. Hold hands. Touch the teeth and hair of your victims before that last kiss. I know you think it's art, what you do, a message to God. It isn't. And you aren't blessed or cursed. You're an amniotic moment of confusion, a blip on the pulsing screen. We name you as we name the terrifying winds of early spring. And we measure you like the stresses of the earth's faults. What makes you worse is the way you stare back, exactly like us, as a mirror sends back the same slow message every day: goodbye; I love you; I will kill you just the same.

Proverbial Zero

I had outgapped you by days and launched a public worship of parking meters. My hum-handed bedshakes made it difficult to light the sea-stars and mirror-wicks. The gnawing time-light crept in until the room smelled of translation. There was no time to evaluate the burn system or the ballet of ice-drawn celebrants beneath simian cloudbursts. Those tendencies toward tarantulas backfired in the squirrel sanctuary. I resorted to the tock and tick of time travel. I unsouled the natives. My jawbone felt its teeth turn to music. I offered a furtive salute to the flag-flapping of the past but the film broke mid-reel. A chasm between the past and future: the Zeno-present where we live in-vitro oblongota. Such a void and lovely blind spot. Now we're chronic.

The Fall of the Empire

Comes like a hammer to a window, a thin crash.
Like a row of bees, angry, through the hole.
Or strange and unwanted, a pained guest,
a guest who has not long to live.

Come slowly, I tell it, and gentle as an evening.
Come unlike a bee sting—serene, harmless,
raining over the house, raining me asleep.
It would be good if it came in my old age like a blue wind

from a nest in the yard. If it came on quick wings by night,
while I slept on the couch, having finished for the day.
Or it would be good if it startled me and was over,
if all at once the sky went dark and the snow

was a cold sting I did not feel. If it came
like the frozen bee I found the other day,
no longer dangerous, but asleep. If it was like sleep,
curled on a rock in the snow. It is only a shell,

I wanted to say, its dead wings still against its husk.
It is only a wing that has stopped against the body, in the cold.
I can put so many names to it, none of them good.
It would be best if it had no wings at all.

Loneliness

Sometimes these boys on the avenue
just want to hang out and talk about guns.
They want to screw their baseball caps on low
and throw rocks at cars. Often, a girl
walks past as though they're not even there,
as though she can't hear them talking
or the sounds of their hands in their pockets.
Snow comes down like a handful of cigarettes.
I have nothing to say to boys like that,
who lean against the gas pumps and spit on the ground.
The bills of their caps shadow their faces
so I can't tell if they're smiling or what.
It could be that they're thinking about theft.
Maybe the wind will steal their voices away.
It is often a long night this time of year
and, far away, someone turns a radio up
so the air is full of the beating of my heart.

Air Disaster Over Kansas

Did a shining god put a kiss on the nosecone?
The airplane rocked on its wings, an engine droned

then coughed. A rotor stopped and would not turn
again. The gas tank burned

and someone saw a creature on the wing
scraping long talons over the singed

flaps, gray head tucked low. I drained
my drink and called the stewardess. *The plane,*

she said, *is going down. Will you have a last*
and final scotch? I would. I gave her all my cash

for which she thanked me, backing queasily
away. The others sat uneasily

craning their dull necks to the windows
as the hungry creature bit the wing. Though

it was little comfort, it occurred to me,
through the stink of smoke and gasoline,

that America loves a doomed and falling
populace, at least as much as it loves anything.

Age of Enlightenment

I rented on Forbes below Mercy.
That was before the dry rot
and patch-plastered lathe
of the Hill sparked and charred

when Dr. King was put down
on a concrete balcony.
It was a straight shot
from front door to footed tub,

four adjoining rooms, no hall.
Upstairs, the roof hatch
hinged onto asphalt,
a running leap

over the sour updraft
of a tomcat alley
to a tarpaper beach
where I'd read sunstunned,

cooled by Newton's proofs
of natural order, a physics
that corrected the Romantic:
slump of chimneys and silver

of trolley tracks
flashing the lip of horizon
as if it were the edge
of a roof or a raft

that contained the world as known.
I looked hard.
Held still.
Read to ride out

the sun's roil, so fierce
that sparrows' wingtips
cast pixilated shadows.
I thought, This is what

Enlightenment is:
full illumination, sum-
total seen and foreseeable.
At dusk I'd cross back,

once a week, call home
to ask how she felt
on the regimen of x-rays
and pills. "Trying to keep it

light," she'd say. I'd listen
past her thready breath
to marrow thinning, bones
fissured with pockets of air,

how she was almost
untethered,
a shadow passing
out of sight.

Scald

Lunchtime when it spilled suddenly
was evening when the flock flies

straight up out of the tree
and she loses her feet because her eyes

are following all the birds at once
scattering into where blue was but isn't

tree heads and chimneys jump out big
before they disappear

when her arm jumped, she was in it
and everything else gone away but Mommy

dabbing, pressing butter on the fire
how many times do I have to

scolding them called it but doctor said
scald

in her earbones she could hear how close
the sounds would come

before she disappeared into their burn

Coronology

A The advantage of bearing an **Asbestos** Crown is that your thoughts always remain perfectly insulated. Never does your brain bubble & burn with bewilderment or ire, nor does your memory freeze up the first time you hit the buzzer during your long-awaited Jeopardy debut. But though the crown itself with its slender curls isn't unattractive, most people tend to avoid your immediate vicinity. As for the members of your family, who must love you no matter what, in your atmosphere they too become cool-headed, though also short-lived.

B A vital aspect of the care of crowns is **balneology**, the science of therapeutic baths. Some crowns thrive from regular immersions in peats & fens; others require solutions of whey, brine, parfin, or liquid gold. A young crown needs a longer bath; an aging crown needs a deeper one. It is necessary to fit the bath to the crown, not the crown to the bath.

C When unfreezing a woman, you must take particular care to thaw her crown at a slower rate than the rest of her body, otherwise it will swell & crack, then melt & drip, swiftly hardening into an adamantine mask. Your next-door-neighbor who never leaves her house?—it's not agoraphobia from which she suffers, but the apparent **calcification** of the Aurora Borealis all over her face, just because *somebody* was in too much of a hurry; *somebody* wasn't willing to take their time.

D This is how the story goes: after the drive-in movie & the sodas at the malt shop, two teenagers sneak away to the woods to park & make out inside the pulsating soundwaves of Top 40 Hits. But just as his fingers reach tremblingly for the top button on her blouse, there comes a newsflash: *Serial killer escaped from the Maximum Security Prison for the Criminally Insane!* The boy wants to leave at once, but the girl convinces him that they should stay. *Just do the* *math*, she says. *The population of our township hovers between 1,432 & 1500; thus, the odds of his encountering the two of us as opposed to any of the others are so minuscule as to be virtually infinitesimal.* They go back to their kissing, and his fingers brush the smooth surface of her second button. But then they hear it: footsteps in the dry leaves, *crunch, crunch, crunch.* Hastily, the boy turns the key in the ignition: *click!* The battery's dead, drained by the aforementioned Top 40 Hits. What to do, what to do? This isn't the kind of story that includes cell phones, so they can't call for help. Desperately, he turns the key again & again: *Click, click, click.* Of course, he knows that's useless, but no doubt you've behaved similarly in like situations. Naturally, for lack of anything better to do, he turns to blaming the girl; after all, she was the one who wanted to stay. But *Uh-UH,* she says, *We ain't gonna be NObody's urban legend!* (Despite the fact that she is not only Caucasian but the palest & blondest of all the xanthochroi ever to grace the shores of Lake Waukesha, when confronted with a challenge, she tends to slip unconsciously into jive talk, which is why she was denied First Place—unfairly, many claim—in the All-County Final Debate, Sophomore Level). She has a plan, but will it work? *Crunch, crunch, crunch.* Switch to the perspective of the serial killer approaching the car. What does he see in the darkness? Two huddled forms in the front seat under their youthful crowns. He reaches in with his hook & slashes at their human softness—but what's this? Something doesn't feel right—where is that satisfying sensation of resistant bone? This is the point in the story where we freeze-frame him as the teenagers tiptoe away to safety while he reaches in to find only their heavy winter coats, & on top, the two now-famous **Decoy** Crowns!

E The **Efficiency** Crown is a diadem of laser beams which you may safely admire from behind welder's goggles, but if you remove them, the lights will penetrate your pupils, searing their image onto the delicate retinal tissue, so that for the rest of your days, you will behold everything as though from behind a veil of dry white light that coldly burns away all the world's impurities, making everything appear textureless & two-dimensional. Your fingertips will assure you that the ridged scar on the back of your beloved's hand is still there, but your eyes won't be able to perceive it. Thus, your senses will remain at war with one another until finally you weary of the conflict, and resolve to either stop looking or stop touching. Sadly, most people choose the latter.

F The temperature inside her **Fenestrated** Crown is always so much higher than that of the surrounding atmosphere that the crown's windows are perpetually frosted over, as if her thoughts are always blushing. On her sixteenth birthday, when she awoke to find her mother bending over her, gently scraping the frost away from the glass with a Rubbermaid spatula, she was so enraged that she jumped right out of bed & walked out the front door in her Laura Ashley nightgown & bare feet, never to return again. The second violation of her crown occurred at the age of 34 when she was still under anesthesia after an emergency appendectomy. Upon waking, she sensed immediately that someone had disturbed her beautiful frost; looking into a hand mirror, she beheld etched upon her crown's windowpanes a garden of snapdragons, harebells, & Sweet William, complete with a honeybee half-drinking, half-drowning in a dew-filled blossom. Was it a nurse who had done this? An aide? Was it a conspiracy that the entire surgical team had participated in like a gang rape while she lay there helpless on the operating table? She sued the hospital (a precedent-setting case in which she represented herself) & won twenty-five million dollars. Thus, we admire but do not necessarily like her.

G According to 1 Samuel 17:49, David's stone struck **Goliath** "in his forehead, so that the stone sank into his forehead, & he fell on his face to the earth." According to the earliest texts, however, what actually happened was that the stone made direct contact with Goliath's *crown*, driving the metal plate right into the giant's skull. No mention of the decapitated head is made after David presented it to Saul, but we know that the skull with its permanently-fused crownplate must be around somewhere; someone would have seen that it was carefully preserved. A few expeditions have sought it, but geopolitical conflict has foiled every one of them. Indiana Jones, where are you?

H Deep in your burrowing place under the blankets, you wake to a racket on the roof that must be announcing the descent of the **Hailstone** Crown, though who's to say for sure? The Hailstone Crown is alarmingly indeterminate, subject to sudden transformations. Maybe even now it's changing to a shower of turkey gizzards, or human gallstones, or wisdom teeth. Tiny magnets shaped like Scottie dogs? Petrified little brides & grooms from all the wedding cakes of history? Silver suitcase keys? Miniature spun-glass beehives? The blazing coals of Isaiah's vision? Or marbles, like so many calcified points of no return—not the elegant Sulphites with their silver doves & swans glowing spectrally at the center, but micro Pee Wees, coreless Lutzes with their gold sparkles searing tiny burn marks in the storm. Or maybe Irish Diamonds, which are really rock crystals, or American Rubies, which are really garnets—no less radiant than authentic gems, but so much more appropriate as a crown for this particular neighborhood.

I Why, that man striding along a few feet ahead of you in the downtown lunchtime crowd *doesn't have a crown!* How brazen, how obscene! Longing to look away, but quite unable to, you follow the vacuum hovering over his head, but right at the curb, precisely between Walk & Don't Walk, it erupts into a geyser of electrum & emeralds, a rich & swirling violence that subsides as swiftly as it appeared, leaving the man's head bare again. This is the rare **Intermittent** Crown, spouting just a few times in the bearer's lifespan—in some cases, only once!, and sometimes (cruelly!) during sleep.

J When the guy with the **Jailbreak** Crown moves to town, all the girls with **Pastry** crowns find him irresistible because each of them is confident that the key in the center of her particular pastry matches the lock in the little steel door in his crown. From behind that door, there's the sound of something that needs to be set free. To one girl, it sounds like a flock of meadow larks all beating their wings at the same time. To another, it sounds like the engine of a rebuilt 1977 Harley FXS LowRider. Whatever it is, it's clearly larger than the brassy cage that confines it. That's why so many girls have sacrificed their one & only key in vain. Even the girl with the

Cupcake Crown was unsuccessful, though inside her dozen cupcakes she had *twelve* keys which fitted pin-tumbler locks, push-key padlocks, locks with revolving cylinders, quadruply wanded locks, spring-latch locks, lever locks, rim locks, Sphinx locks, Tibetan locks, chastity locks, the final lock of the Sacred Brotherhood of the Order of Freemasonry, & the infamous White Gold Lock of New Delhi. It's gotten so that he pulls down the shades & refuses to answer the door whenever he sees a pastry girl coming up the sidewalk. He did perk up a little at the visit of the girl with the **Rum Flambe** Crown & a key too hot to touch, but when they got the key out with tongs, it turned out to be as useless as all others. O, that rumbling from inside his crown! O, those ravaged cakes!

K Because a poet's vocation is to make everything difficult that is easy, & vice versa, the **Knotted** Crown becomes him or her with its convoluted cluster of filigreed intertwinings. Anyone near the poet must resist the temptation to trace & retrace the various loops & turnings in order to locate the starting point of any of the designs. Sometimes when a parent notices knots beginning to develop on a child's crown, that parent attempts to file, scrape, or sand them off, or, as in recent news, sear them off with a blow torch. Such endeavors are, of course, illegal, though not incomprehensible.

L A **Lone-Standing** Crown makes everyone uneasy. Why didn't the crown choose to share its bearer's fate, whatever it may have been? That's why in many provinces the crown of a deceased person must consign itself to the flames in order to prove its loyalty. Any crown that refuses to do so is ritually destroyed by the crowd. There are a few bearers who add to their wills the controversial **clause of coronal manumission**, setting their crowns free upon their demise, but the prevailing opinion is that a lone-standing crown is a vulnerable crown, & therefore potentially treacherous, even if only by example, so that kindest & most socially responsible act is to take the crown with one into the afterlife.

M **Migraines** are the pangs of crownbirth, the teething of uncut diamonds as they break through. See also **febrile chills, auras, swooning, & temporal distortions.**

N When you see someone whose hair has gone Lamentations White & whose crown gapes emptiness where the ruby ought to be, offer a prayer of thanks. This is the **Necrotic** Crown, a testament to survival. Though the rotting ruby has been sliced out, the bearer refuses to fill the setting with colored glass, as if to proclaim, *I have sojourned between the lands of the living & the dead—I've returned, I am home, & I wanted you to know.*

O As a rule, the only kind of person who will marry the bearer of an **Osculated** Crown is a narcissist.

P How delicate are the fossilized bones of **Paleolithic** crowns! The archeologist fears that the touch of even the narrowest brush will cause them to disintegrate. It's best to move on to a different zone of the dig site, & seek the campfire markings & pottery shards that are the purpose of the excavation. After dark, though, everyone gathers silently around the bones to marvel at their luminescence.

Q The danger of falling in love with the bearer of a **Quintet** Crown is that you can never be certain whether it's the actual person you desire or the hovering circlet of tiny instrumentalists in black sitting up with impeccable posture on folding chairs & nodding almost imperceptibly to one another as they pass the countermelodies back & forth. Ironically, the danger of falling in love with the bearer of a **Quietness** Crown is exactly the same, though for the opposite reason.

R Three women sit around a kitchen table discussing Madge, who's had to be hospitalized because her crown's **resin canals** have developed blockages resulting in painful dryness & scaling, but when one of the husbands walks in, they immediately change the subject, of course, since that's exactly the kind of thing husbands don't need to hear about.

S Normally, a **Sunken** Crown dissolves on its own within the human body, but when a patient comes in complaining of heaviness & inertia, the physician must perform various harmonic & metallurgical diagnostics to test for the presence of any tenacious crown vestiges. The nature of the remedy depends on the location of the crown residue; a gentle tapping (12/4) time with an ivory mallet will dislodge any gold in the joints, for instance, whereas emerald shards in the throat require a potion of bee venom & molasses. If any part of the crown lodges in the heart, the treatment is homeopathic: the sufferer must sit with his or her chest pressed against a stereo speaker transmitting the saddest music of his/her thirteenth year until disintegration occurs, releasing the internal pressure.

T **Trepannation** is the ancient art of chiseling or drilling holes in the human head in order to cure certain diseases, particularly, homesickness on the part of the crown. However, a crown has never been known to successfully return to the darkness from which it emerged. Like the rest of us, it must continue to, metaphorically speaking, rise & shine; it must continue to not only exist, but to be aware of its existence. It must continue to endure its own glory.

U It is tragic how swiftly television viewers have gotten used to seeing the crowds of Palestinian women on the news, every one of them wearing the **Ululation** Crown.

V Not **volcanoes** but coral atolls crown the South Seas. Thus, every volcano aspires to become an atoll. In one sense, you could describe the atoll as the afterlife of the volcano, but in another sense, the process is not so simple, since it involves a certain degree of overlapping & simultaneity as the volcanic island sinks while the coral skeletons & the algae strain phototropically upward. If the atoll retains any memories from its previous existence, they have long since been filtered through the reflections of clouds in water, all their fury now muted, mere "experience recollected in tranquility."

W Never attempt to iron a **wrinkled** crown. Your mind must adjust to the puckers, the ripples, the ridges, the creased folds. To flatten the crown would be like steam-pressing the brain. Not every surface in the world is meant to be smooth & featureless. When you find yourself frustrated by your wrinkled crown or the wrinkled crown of someone near you, just remind yourself that it is a relief map of reality.

X The introverted response to the presence of a **Xenobiotic** Crown may include headaches, breathlessness, appetite loss, & hyperventilation. The extroverted response generally takes the form of that manic leaping & twirling known as "tarantism"—it is as if the sufferer is trying to "dance off" the crown. Only once has this been known to be successful: in thirteenth century Germany, the stomping & jumping of a crowd of afflicted persons caused a wooden bridge to collapse into the river below. As the dancers were swept away in the swift spring waters, their crowns could be seen slipping from their heads to sink to the stony bottom.

Y Though the waiters had long since cleared the remains of the shrimp-&-cream-lobster-bisque-simmered-in-Madeira, & the wax tapers had burned cleanly down their braided cotton wicks, she had not once interrupted him or even glanced away. But he was constitutionally unable to notice the occasional delicate flaring of her surreptitiously **yawning** crown.

Z A collective rather than an individual illumination, the **Zeitgeist** Crown's appearance depends on its chronological, latitudinal, & longitudinal coordinates. In France during the reign of the Sun King, for instance, it glittered, a chandelier made entirely of ice crystals, its beauty a consequence of the velocity at which it continuously threatened to fall. Now we wear the shadow of the **Reticular** Crown encircling the earth like a fine mesh as we study to decide if it makes us beautiful.

Brother/Sister

At school, Brother and Sister are taught English, although the language their parents speak at home is a harsher tongue. Mother and Father belong to a religious cult that believes that war and electricity are evil. There are taboos against permed hair, patterned cloth, and pneumatic tires for tractors. The school doesn't teach geography or history, for these subjects present the outside world, with its wars, intrigues, and technology. The teacher won't teach fairy tales or myths; she objects to stories that aren't true, such as those in which animals talk and act like people, or stories that involve magic. Reading material must not glorify physical force, nationalism, militarism, or modern technology. Each story should teach a moral; those that are just nice are not good enough.

Brother and Sister learn how to add. Some of you girls may marry men who aren't so good with figures, the teacher says. You'll need to know how to help along with the figuring.

The teacher doesn't much care for the scientific method. Brother and Sister love the scientific method. Brother wants to cut up animals and corpses and see what makes them work. The teacher rarely paddles children; only for lying or cheating or vulgar language or smutty talk. Only for open disobedience or physically dangerous activity, such as running into the highway or teasing a nervous buggy horse.

Brother and Sister sneak out to the barn at night. In a secret cubbyhole, they've hidden a battery-operated radio. They listen to the music, and they act like singers. They dance; they act like crazy children, and like prisoners. Brother conducts experiments. He finds a dead cat by the highway and uses his radio to reanimate it with electricity. He cuts the cat's brain in two. He believes the English of his secret biology textbook is what his teacher means by vulgar language and smutty talk.

Listen, Sister, he says. Cutting the neural connections between one half of the brain and the other is useful to control the flurries of random electrical activity that cause epileptic fits.

Sister says, I am so impressed and delighted with all your smutty talk.

Sister says, You shall be a doctor and I shall be a nurse.

But Brother graduates from eighth grade and his schooling is over. He helps with the chickens and the pigs and learns something more useful than all day book-learning. At school, Sister is alone with her chalkboards and chalk.

At night, they journey. While the other children of the family lie asleep and dreaming, they travel through the blue moonlight or the hushed, severe dark if there is no moon. In the moonlight, the farm looks like it was infused with a luminous powder from another world. The barn is enchanted.

Brother examines the map of a corpse, from an old anatomy book.

It's time to sow your wild oats, says Sister. Don't you want to put an engine in your buggy and snort cocaine?

Brother just grunts and traces the path of some artery with his finger.

Or get a paper route? asks Sister. And spend the profits on some prohibited form of transportation? A moped, or a speed boat perhaps?

These are my wild oats, says Brother, gesturing to indicate the severed cat's brain, the radio, and his collage of biology and anatomy photos. I want to go to high school. I want to go to college and then medical school.

But he only gathers the eggs and feeds the chicks and sneaks out at night to read his outdated biology books and cut up dead animals. He develops dark circles under his eyes, and a dazed look, as if he is wandering through a dream. Sister is also suffering from sleep deprivation. As she copies ridiculous verses off the board at school over and over again she begins to hallucinate. The letters seem to blur together into an animated monster of scribbles, a living script telling the same story over and over again, a story of sacrificial death.

Then it is time to be baptized. This cult is called Anabaptist, because they think baptizing babies is wrong. In the old days, Anabaptists were tortured and martyred because they wouldn't take their babies down by the river. They wouldn't dip them in the water. The minister tells Brother and Sister and the other youth all about these fabulous martyrs and their exquisite torment. He shows them illustrations from a heavy book. Brother and Sister jump right in the river. Sister feels something new; she feels surrounded by a warm presence like God or science or music.

The country is at war. People come home from this war with bizarre ailments, not all of them rooted in reality. An epidemic has erupted of racking coughs and painful bleeding sores. Brother must do some mandatory "voluntary service", to avoid killing people. He serves and studies in a hospital and Sister comes along and studies to be a nurse.

Sister meets a man who is also a member of the cult. He is growing his first stubble, not yet thick enough to hide the fact that he is soft. He is so much daintier than the rest of the farm boys, as if he is the sort of man people mean when they talk about strangers. He loves to prepare picnic baskets and take Beth out to the meadow, where he draws ornate scenarios in his sketchbook. Beth is lively and gay; she talks and she sings with this man, and she takes her long, lustrous hair out from underneath its covering. Her boyfriend is stunned. Never have I seen such beautiful hair, he says, and he begins to sketch her.

But then he goes off to Greece for his own voluntary service. In Greece, there is an accident. The lake is deep or bottomless or disturbing: pale and green. He is riding along on his bike, but is hit by a car and hurled into the lake. He drowns. Whenever Sister talks about it, she says, *He drowned in the country of Greece*, to avoid saying, *He drowned in Greece*. She doesn't want anyone to think that he drowned in an enormous vat at McDonalds.

Now that your lover is dead, Beth's parents tell her, you can come live with us on the farm again. If your lover's death proved anything, it is the dangers and evils of modern transportation. Speed kills; the world is not for you. Maybe Brother is off in the world studying to be a doctor and to use electricity and other sinful components of the modern world—cars, cameras, heart fibrillators—but he is a boy. Boys are different, as is self-evident.

She works quietly alongside her parents on the farm. Her father's beard grows long and white. He sits in his rocking chair, which is made out of thin canes of wood like whips, and he rocks. The rocking chair is gnarled and scrubby and the old man is gnarled and scrubby. He rarely speaks in his harsh, Germanic language, but Mother interprets his silences and his monosyllables for Sister, and Sister only listens. He is communicating his apprehensions about technological progress and the loss of community. He is insisting on humility, simple living, and resignation to do the will of God. The Bible is open in his lap; he mumbles something, and nods off. He meant that we are strangers in this land, Mother says.

She quotes the Bible, where God is very angry and kicks the man and the woman and the snake out of the garden. He curses them all. He tells the snake that he will bite men's feet and that men will hit him on the head. He tells the woman that she will be subordinate and that she will suffer much pain in childbearing. He tells the man that it will be nothing but work and thistles and death as he scratches his meager living from the dust to which he shall return.

Sister believes that the chicken house is full of snakes. It is her job to enter this long narrow building and gather the eggs. As soon as the baby male chicks are hatched, it is her job to dump them in a heap back behind the building. The building has no windows; it is lined with enormous fans. The sun is blazing. On the top layer of corpses, insects are eating the eyeballs of some still-living chicks. Sometimes Father grinds them up to use as fertilizer on the fields. One day she is wandering across the earth and she comes across a screeching baby chick with no legs or wings that is somehow still alive. Just a beak, really; shrieking, shrieking, shrieking. Sister thinks it is the most horrifying and true and beautiful song she has ever heard.

Brother has made it in the world. Now that he's a doctor, he can cut up dead things whenever he wants. But he feels he is missing something. Cutting up dead things isn't enough. He writes the family letters, and Mother reads them out loud, as Father dozes in his rocking chair. I sometimes feel as if I'm being suffocated by a vast living organism, Brother writes. The world. The world makes me uneasy, just as Mother and Father and the teachers always said it would. Back home, everything is peaceful, segmented, and subdued. Here in the city it is all pulsing, beating, a never-ending vastness of tissues.

Mother sighs, contented.

Mother writes back to Brother in her wobbly script, and asks everyone else to do the same, all the vague and busy and inbred siblings and cousins who live on identical farms in the surrounding countryside. Mother will scrutinize Sister's letter to Brother, and then shove it in an envelope full of letters. Sister can only write in code. I remember the good clean fun we used to have playing in the barn! she writes. Sometimes I think I have never had such fun! Remember when we pretended we were prisoners? Oh, how silly children are. Please come visit soon, for I would like to escape from my pleasant chores for just one afternoon talking with you about how good God is and the joys of living on the farm!

But Brother doesn't come. He thinks it is just those exclamation points that give Sister's writing such a hysterical tone.

Sister grows desperate. This is no life. She runs out to the highway that passes her farm, and removes her hair covering. Her lustrous hair blows in the wind. A passing car slams on its brakes, and the driver beckons her to join him. His name is Daniel, and he has a cult of his very own. He calls himself the Church of Christ with the Elijah Message. He drives her across the endless plains in his sinful car, and they spend the night in a dilapidated hotel that rises from the plains like the rotted carcass of some ancient and monstrous life form. She wakes in the night and lights a candle and wanders the endless halls in her nightgown. The hotel has more levels than she would have supposed possible; it seems infinite. She feels vaguely disturbed, as if there is something wrong with her own size.

The next day, he drives her to the Ozarks, where they will live with his mother and be safe from the coming apocalypse. His mother is a silent woman with bushy eyebrows and a tendency toward indecipherable muttering. Sister grows a light mustache. When the mother dies, God communicates with her husband. God tells her husband that he can bring her back. He shoves his mother's body in the refrigerator freezer and announces to the world the impending miracle.

In River City, Brother sees these things on television.

Isn't this a crazy world? his patients ask him.

I do not know what this world looks like, says Brother.

I have a problem with my stomach, his patients say.

There is something rotten stuck in my intestines, his patients say.

Everything I consume is disgusting, his patients say.

He examines them thoroughly.

There is nothing wrong with your innards, he says. But maybe you should have your brain examined.

He explains that the brain is composed of two lobes, and that the relationship between these two lobes is poorly understood. Somewhere in the communication between the dominant half and the other half lies the problem of their indigestion.

Sister has been quiet for many years. Her parents no longer speak to her, because they want her to see that the man she married is a wicked man and the life she lives is a wicked life. She has worked alongside her crazy husband, who is a charlatan, without speaking. Come to think of it, she has never spoken. She has never said a thing, except in their childhood. She remembers the elaborate scenarios they acted out at night in the barn. They imagined strangers, it seems, who would break all the rules. They imagined bizarre ways of giving birth; they imagined journeys by ship and by train. They told magical stories which they imagined would change them, and transform the farm.

Only once in her life did she speak in the daylight, to that boy who drowned in the country of Greece.

Sister gets a job as a nurse. Every day she works at the hospital and every day she drives out to a farm after work to buy eggs and every day she drives past a lake. She thinks about that one who loved her. If he had never died she would have married him and she never would have married this crazy man who tried to raise his mother from the dead. She never would have been shunned by Mother and Father.

At the hospital, her patients complain that they have no will to live. They have hysterical pregnancies and miscarriages and give birth to deformed fetuses. They complain that the doctor doesn't love them, and that they've been locked up in coffins. Brother doesn't speak anymore either. He thinks that these people from the bad part of town, from down by the river, who complain and complain and complain about their imaginary ailments are just too much. He speaks to them as little as possible, but he writes them prescriptions for pills. He drives away in his long, black car.

Sister calls up on the phone.

How are our parents? she asks.

Who knows? says Brother. I can't call them up on the phone, because they believe telephones are evil. I can drive to see them in my long, black car, but it is a difficult journey from River City out to the farm where they live and I get so tired of the way they think my car is evil. They write letters to me in their wobbly script because their hands tremble so, but it has been several months since I heard word from them.

At least you aren't shunned, says Sister.

Brother shrugs. There is a long silence. Sister can't remember how to speak to Brother the way she did as a child. All she can think of is code. Everything. Everything is just a code.

You should come to visit me, says Sister. You really should come to visit.

Your husband makes me nervous, says Brother.

Please come, says Sister.

I'll see what I can do, says Brother.

Sister has nothing more to say, and Brother has nothing more to say. In their heads, they keep talking. When their story is over, they'll never speak again.

Sister is sadder every day. Her crazy husband tells her the apocalypse will start next month, according to one or another incarnation of Elijah. The final battle is coming and Satan will be cast out. What most other charlatans and evangelical lunatics don't understand, he tells her, is that Satan is inside the whole human race. The human race is a symbiotic organism. There are no good people and no bad people, no chosen sheep and black ones, no wheat and no chaff. The evil half has to be burned out of every last human. Everyone will be burnt simultaneously from the inside—they will all suffer together through unimaginable pain as an entire 50% of their souls is seared out of their very being. Like a lobotomy without anaesthetic.

And then they will be beings of light alone.

Interesting theory, thinks Sister, from a man who put his own mother inside a refrigerator and told the world he would bring her back from the dead. Sister is depressed.

One day, after picking up the eggs, she drives down to the lake and she gets out and walks around the lake and she sees that it is nice and deep, or even bottomless. The water is murky and blackish and green. She gets back in her car and she drives right in. The car sinks to the bottom and the water rushes in the open window.

Some friendly people see her drive in, people who believe in life. They fish her out, and they fish the eggs out too. They call a policeman, who wraps her in a warm blanket and chats with her in his car. His ass is so flat, as if he's been sitting on cushions and chatting his whole lifetime long.

It's a marvel, he says. These eggs weren't damaged at all.

Did you drive in there on purpose? he asks.

Sister doesn't answer. She is shivering and dazed.

I'm just asking, he says. I know you are a good church girl, and suicide is a crime.

I guess I must have fallen asleep at the wheel, Sister says. I guess I didn't look where I was going.

The cop drops her off back at home where her husband is waiting.

The next week, she borrows her husband's car to drive to work. It is a long shift, all through the night. The night is dark and full of stars and the night at the hospital is full of people with many ailments, people who complain that they have swallowed something rotten or that they cannot smell. The hospital is shaped like intestines and it is full of fluorescent lights which make the sick people look even worse. Nobody becomes well in this hospital. Instead, their sicknesses grow more convoluted, to resemble the hospital itself. She wanders through these hallways, up and down circular and grey flights of stairs, and it occurs to her that she could never find the end of this place. She ducks into a room where a thin girl with a deathly complexion and a swelling belly is muttering and sobbing.

I swallowed something shiny and hard, the girl says. And now I'm going to have a baby.

That isn't exactly possible, Sister explains.

Stop raping me, says the girl.

Sister doesn't know what is happening. She is overwhelmed by the strangest feeling. She identifies with this sad girl to the point she's not sure which of them is which. Which of them the patient and which of them the nurse. Sister opens the girl's chart and reads it at random. In her latest understanding of her childhood, it says of the girl, her father's sexual appetite is insatiable and omnivorous. Despite the false aspects of the life history she tells, no one doubts the seriousness of her behavior or her continued threats to hurt herself.

When she gets off work, Sister drives home. It is early morning and her husband is still sleeping. He opens his eyes as if registering a particularly vivid dream, and closes them again. The mist rises from the river back in the trees and lies low to the ground like a ghostly shroud. She writes him a note.

I have gone to get the eggs, it says.

She pauses, wondering if she meant to say something else. Perhaps she could have written: You are just another bleak and tangy surface of the material world. There is nothing in your pungent flesh to tempt me anymore. I moved beyond you long ago. It is only the after-image, the burn on your retina, which writes to you now.

She decides that "I have gone to get the eggs" will do.

She drives to the lake. There is nobody around, there is nobody watching. She drives right in. She drives right in and she sinks down in her husband's car, which rests down there now next to the car she drove in the week before. The water rushes into the car and the water rushes into her lungs.

Many of the people who knew her, who dislike her crazy husband, are suspicious: maybe her evil husband drove her in that lake himself or at least drove her to do it. In the newspaper, her co-workers are quoted to this effect. They emphasize her mysterious bruises. Her patients are quoted, including the sad girl with the swelling belly. The emphasis there is on her kindness and appropriate care. Brother is quoted as well. He remembers her as a girl, so lively and gay. Although everyone has a slightly different interpretation, everyone agrees that she is in a better place. Everyone agrees that she is better off now than when she was alive.

Sleep

A baby cries, a sound that digs in.

That will not stop without intervention.

On and on.

My sleep is a thrown spear, a dive, a body displacing its weight in green water.

Asleep, I am shucked clean. I belong to no one.

The 2nd Mike lies on his back, dug in, waiting me out. What I wouldn't give for 8 hours, he frequently says. He has offered to pay me, topping off at $100. But I'm holding out for the really big cash.

A parking ticket's 50 bucks! the1st Mike once said. He was double parked. This was years ago. You have to make adjustments, fifty dollars then—vs—fifty dollars now.

I walked across the bed on my knees, reaching for buckles and lapels.

He said, Fifty bucks! How could it be worth it?, but of course he didn't go.

You go! I say to the 2nd Mike, fighting wakefulness: the sound of my voice, the sound of the crying of the baby. It's your turn!

A bottle in the fridge.

A blanket on the floor.

A kick, a tweak, a shudder.

We had a deal, I say. Take your shift!

He shifts. He is wearing a Walkman, dead to the girl clamor: the baby, me. Noise must be pitched to the feminine ear. Sleep must be a man thing. His sleep goes deep, but mine is a hot knife through butter.

You know I need more sleep than you! this Mike says. You can get by on less.

He says, Can't you just let me!

He closes his eyes.

He does not hear telephones or hail storms or the baby. Me calling out with occasional nightmares.

He once slept through a fire, he told me: the smoke, the heat, the sound effects. Or that might have been the other Mike.

This Mike isn't moving: eyes deep-socketed, willed to stillness.

The sour inward grump of his breath.

A dim mutter that is the sound of the voice from the Walkman.

I elbow his shoulder; his shoulder rocks forward, then back—dead to the world, or just dead.

I have a black dress, a black hat, a picture of temperate grief. I believe in preparation.

My sister and I slept in the same bed when we were little—dirty feet, twisted nightgowns, the faint occasional whiff of dried pee. The rhythm of the breathing of the one was the rhythm of the breathing of the other. We were growing our hair. It tangled across the pillows, coming from her head or mine.

The 2nd Mike, when I met him, had a boy's bed, the kind a boy slept in: poled knees, tented covers. I was between Mikes, or between intentions: the Mikes overlapped. I snuck out and called the 2nd Mike from phonebooths. Going out for ice cream, I told the 1st Mike, then I came home with my fingers sticky.

I never slept. Took taxis back and forth in the middle of the night.

I need more sleep than you do! says the 2nd Mike, this is in the morning in the wake of his most recent failure to wake. We are fighting over our exhaustion. My arm is asleep from the weight of the baby.

You know me! He says.

A deep sleeper.

A Walkman.

I am a bristled ball, a ball tripping sparks, distorting light and subject and the scent of potpourri in rooms.

You know I sleep more soundly than you do!

He follows me from room to room as I do this and this and this. Sheets snap. Baby spoons clatter from the baby's high chair. His toenails scrape the backs of my heels.

Once he got up in the night; once or twice or three times. Went to her room, dimly lit by a green glass butterfly nightlight. Picked her up, put her down, rocked her, walked her. The crying went on and on, a car alarm you wait for the relief of the end of.

The floor creaked under the rocking chair runners.

Under the weight of his back-and-forth feet.

I waited for the sound of the end of the crying.

He came to the doorway with the baby.

She doesn't want me, he said, lit only to the waist by the glow from her butterfly nightlight.

My sister and I slept like kittens, like a basket of snakes. Our cheeks bore the marks of each other's fingers. One's hair knotted into the hair of the other. Our mother used scissors to cut the knots out.

I have to get some sleep! I said in the days of the 2nd Mike's small bed.

I liked things then that I never liked: heat, spicy foods, the lateness of the hour. We ate in all-night diners or in Cuban sandwich bars or Taquerias: black beans, pigeon peas, things I didn't know the names of. We kissed on dark corners and spilled sugar on the tables.

I got hives.

I got ridges in the surface of my nails.

I abandoned sleep as I abandoned all else: daylight, health, the first Mike.

I did things I never did.

Come and get me, this Mike says. If I fall asleep in the living room? Wake me up. I just don't hear her. Is that my fault?

I didn't know: was it?

We tried things, do-it-yourselfers. Moved the crib. Changed soaps. Put a higher watt bulb in the butterfly nightlight.

We bought a nursery monitor. Set it on the nightstand on the Mike's side of the bed. I tuned it high so it could be heard over the sound of the Walkman: the crying a siren, her breathing a mechanical rasp I heard through the two pillows over my head, but not this

Mike.

He hung on. In the morning he said, Was it my imagination or did she sleep through the night?

I went to see a doctor for the hives, the ridges, certain inflammations.

I am concerned, the doctor said. Hepatitis? Jaundice? Didn't like the color of the whites of my eyes.

I showed him the places where the hives came out, but he kept tugging at my eyelids

I laughed. I said, I'm fine.

I said, You're a dermatologist!

I said, It's lack of sleep. When I'm tired this is the color the whites of my eyes are.

He shook his head, writing something, zipping something off a pad.

Seriously, he said. Here is the name of a lab. This should be seen to.

I missed funerals. I missed doctor's appointments. I missed hours I was not allowed to miss at my job so I could stay in the small bed with the 2nd Mike. We slept past the sound of other people's alarms and showers and toast, eggs, coffee in the morning, into the sound of recess at the school across the street, the clatter of children like a spill of coal into a pan. We ate at odd hours. The diner served breakfast round-the-clock.

When we were bigger, my sister and I, we were separated: two beds, two rooms. I am told that we slept with our heads against the common wall like Siamese twins, but then I turned. Sometimes I looked up and there she was in the doorway in the middle of the night—a spectral color, the spectral shiver of her nightgown at her feet. She said it was me who woke her, calling out with nightmares, but neither one remembered in the morning.

Tell me we will always be like this, said the 2nd Mike, fierce. He left bruises in the shape of butterflies under the skin on my arms.

He meant the spark and the whistle. Tongues on dark corners. Fingers dipped in spilled sugar at the table in the diner.

He meant things involving Vaseline and oil in the dark.

No tepid pauses.

No sad creases in the pants.

He meant, our mouths gone sore.

He meant, fingering the soreness.

He meant, the bed, the radio, us clicking in the shadowed light of the tv.

Now, all he covets is sleep.

That kind of bruising, said the doctor fingering the butterfly bruises on my arm. Bruising can be a symptom. That should be checked.

This Mike is asleep on the couch again, pulled up, eyes hip-hopping. The tv has been going all night. The nursery monitor is on the floor near the couch.

CAN'T YOU GIVE ME A BREAK! CAN'T YOU SEE HOW TIRED I AM! His voice is sudden. His face goes from the color of sleep to the color of bruises.

I jump. The baby jumps in my arms. I am sometimes afraid of things he might do.

I say, Go to sleep earlier!

I say, Sleep in the bedroom!

I say, I'm tired too! I get up every two hours every night! What do you do?

Exhaustion blues the air.

He says, WHY IS IT ALWAYS A CONTEST? WHY IS IT ALWAYS ABOUT YOU? CAN'T YOU JUST CONCEDE YOU NEED LESS SLEEP THAN I DO?

I was afraid my sister was cutting my hair in the middle of the night. One's was long and one's was longer. It was a contest. Or there was something else about me that she hated.

Sometimes, in the morning, my hair seemed shorter. Jagged. Alop. Though she was stealthy and careful. I never found the scissors, and there were never any snippings on the sheets.

I can't fucking stand it! he says, awakened for once by the crying in the night. He sits on the side of the bed in the posture of dressing. This apartment has never been empty of Mikes. I hear the crying doubled up. The living room is empty, except for the sound of the crying.

He says he doesn't hear it.

He says he needs sleep.

In the middle of the night, I am sometimes afraid of what he might do.

I'm so fucking exhausted, he says.

He says, It's too fucking noisy to sleep here!

He says, I would leave if I had some other place to go to.

Outside the airshaft of the room with the small bed, somebody watched sex videos, the oh oh oh tripping along through the night.

Somebody had a late picnic.

Somebody, coughing, cried.

Somebody had a printer so loud and insistent it interfered with the rhythm of my breath.

I needed quiet. I needed sleep. I went home in the dark in a taxi. By then, the 1st Mike was rarely there and when he was, he was not the 1st Mike.

He bristled, he tripped sparks, he altered light and the sound waves in rooms.

Where have you been?

Who have you been with?

What have you been doing?

I answered what I could. I said the names of foods, the names, I thought, of least betrayal: black beans, pigeon peas.

Mexican food? The 1st Mike said. Mexican food? You don't like Mexican food! You never eat Mexican food with me!

I couldn't sleep. I was sometimes afraid of what he might do in the middle of the night.

The hives persisted. The symptoms of jaundice. Nothing helped.

I left the country: this was in the days of the 2nd Mike's small bed.

In the days when the 1st Mike was present, but absent.

Most of the crying was done by me.

My passport photo was in black-and-white and did not show the butterfly bruises or the off-white tint of the whites of my eyes.

The 1st Mike drove me to the airport, but it was the 2nd Mike I called, waking him up across time zones.

Can you call back? he said. I'm dead here.

Sleeping pills, my sister said over the phone.

Just try, she said before I could hang up. I'm mailing them Fedex. They work for me.

You take them?

She said, I have always been wakeful. Wandering around in the middle of the night.

There were only four pills, like a trial pack of cigarettes, tucked into a little blue Tiffany's box.

They're perfectly safe, she said when I called to tell her she had successfully mailed drugs across state lines.

She said, I take them.

She said, Do you think I'd give you something that would harm you?

You'll just be asleep, she said. You'll just slide right under.

I went out for walks while the 2nd Mike slept, pale and sun-deprived in the bed that he never made. I was drifting back towards daylight. The 1st Mike was mostly gone, though he was the Mike I meant when I called out in the middle of the night.

The bruises on my arms had begun to disappear. Day, as it turned out, is what I was missing.

You're the parent too, I say, over the crying, over the pale green light from the butterfly nightlight.

He says, I thought it would be different. I thought you were someone who stayed up all night!

I say, That was you.

I say, Now there is a child.

I say, I can't do this alone. Well, I can. But I don't want to.

I try, he says.

You don't. You don't even sleep in the bedroom, where you could possibly hear her.

I can't sleep! he says. I can't get started. If I could get started!

I give him the sleeping pills from years ago, the ones that might have been tainted by my sister. She could have dipped them in poison. Used a q-tip or a paintbrush.

I searched for those scissors but she never left a trace.

He just swallows them down.

I wake in the dark in the bed that is empty of Mikes, afraid of what might have happened.

It is very quiet.

The sound of the crying is a coating.

The absence of the crying is a sound.

The things we have done in the middle of the night.

The tv is off, the living room is empty, nobody answers when I call, Mike.

He is asleep on the floor of the baby's room, his fingers stuck through the bars of the crib, his face frosted in the glow from the butterfly nightlight. The rhythm of the breathing of the one is the rhythm of the breathing of the other.

As it turns out, company was what she wanted.

The Blue The

I.

Then came the wake robin, the skin
of the lake, the bluejay's solitude,
the very beginning of Blue. Then the Blue
Adam was lowered and given an axe. Eve
was carved from his thigh. Then came the Blue Cane,
the Blue Abel, the Blue Enoch, the Blue Irad
and so on to the murderer, the blue Blue Lamech
before the Blue Seth was born.
Then came the Blue Monks dreaming of spoons.
Then came the Blue Merchants dreaming of spoons.
Then came the Blue Doctors dreaming of spoons.

II.

of the tusks of the beast of the island without music
of the reckonings and the gaps of the dreams
of the pleasure of the boats of the river without harbors
of the aisles and the columns of the world
of the five mile grin of the gristle of the fat of the beast
of the swords of the chorus of the hymn
of the first year of disease of the beast
of the stitch of the rupture of the cheek
of the blacksmith's wrists of the printmaker's nostrils
of the shadows of the wasps of the chapel
of the why of the prayer of the heaven
of the broken-armed prophet of the stain of the glass
of the anvil of the flesh of the spirit of the beast

III.

We moved through the world like blue water,
the blue man tells his daughter. The shipwrecked
kicked and reached because they had no choice.
Some came to shore screaming with salt on their breaths,
some went quietly into the hills. Then earth was cleared
for a church and people went to the Blue John to be dipped
in the blue light of the river cutting through the valley
like a bolt of blue lightning. Then we walked along the river
bank before sunrise, our crickets like souls in a casket,
with the earthworms in the Blue Father's tackle-box.
Absolute darkness except for the hooks of blue. We came to
a village with no word for blue. They did not have a blue
With or blue The. They did not have a blue Was. But
by Sunday the small flames of their lamps were blue.

The Blue Castro

You might die before Castro.
You might die and Castro
will still be shepherding himself
into a room striped with bars
to unlace his boots
and set them beside his rifle
which leans in the corner
like a cane. You might be famous
to no one but pallbearers.
The girl who lay her head
upon your lap when you were 17
will be thinking you have passed
only in the way the past can
pass: a folded name,
a doodle of yellowing hearts.
She will be the middle-aged
woman who pays no attention to news
concerning the boat people of Cuba
or the boat people you are among,
scorched by mystified light;
ferried from the shore
by a man-sized crow who uses its wings
as oars. Castro will not lie
awake listening to the moonlight
construct an arch across the sea.
He will lie awake listening
to his young watchmen gossip
in the courtyard. Remember
wandering into homes
before you were lost, a lover's
siblings drifting from room to room.
When you'd descend the trellis
of her thighs, no one seemed to care.
The Late Show buzzed somewhere,
her father dosed, his ear

against the wall. Through the girl's
body you could hear the host's
cruel jokes about the solitude
of Castro, a dictator afraid
of the dark. You might die
the same death as Castro, the bulb
above your bed casting out
the stars. You might be alone
with a fortune-teller who refuses
to talk. Pallbearers might carry you
like a famished emperor,
and leave you brooding
in a meadow like an empty box.

CONTRIBUTORS

Claire Bateman is the author of four books of poems, including *Friction* (winner of the Eighth Mountain Poetry Prize for 1998), and *Clumsy*, (New Issues Press, 2003). She lives in Greenville, South Carolina.

Stephen Beachy is the author of two novels, *The Whistling Song* and *Distortion*. His short fiction and novel excerpts have also been published in *Fourteen Hills*, *Bomb*, *Best Gay American Fiction 1996*, *The Chicago Review*, *The Arsenal pulp Press anthology CONTRA/Dictions*, and *High Risk 2*. He lives in California.

Michael Burkard's available books of poems are *Pennysylvania Collection Agency* (New Issues), *Unsleeping* (Sarabande), *Entire Dilemma* (Sarabande), and *My Secret Boat* (W.W. Norton). He teaches in the MFA program at Syracuse University.

Lewis Buzbee is the author of *Fliegelman's Desire*. His writing has appeared in *Harper's*, *GQ*, *Paris Review*, *ZYZZYVA*, *Best American Poetry*, and elsewhere. He teaches in the MFA program at the University of San Francisco.

Tina Chang's poems have appeared in *Ploughshares*, *Quarterly West*, *The Missouri Review*, *Indiana Review* and *Sonora Review*, among many others. Her poems have been anthologized in *Identity Lessons*, *Poetry Nation*, and *Asian American Literature*. She is the recipient of a 2003 poetry grant from the New York Foundation for the Arts. Her first collection of poetry, *Half-Lit Houses*, is forthcoming from Four Way Books.

Paula Cisewski's poems have appeared in *Conduit*, *Fuori*, *Swerve*, *The Comstock Review*, and in a chapbook, *How Birds Work*, published by Fuori Editions.

Kevin Clark's book, *In The Evening Of No Warning*, recently earned a publisher's grant from the Greenwall Fund of the Academy of American Poets. He teaches modern literatures and creative writing at Cal Poly in San Luis Obispo, where he lives with his wife and two children.

Cynie Cory's first book of poems, *American Girl*, is forthcoming from New Issues Press. New poems have recently appeared in *Black Warrior Review* and *Jacket*.

Jim Daniels' forthcoming books include *Show and Tell: New and Selected Poems* (University of Wisconsin Press), and a new collection of short stories, *Detroit Tales* (Michigan State University Press).

Nancy Eimers has published two collections of poems, *Destroying Angel* (Wesleyan) and *No Moon* (Purdue). She teaches at Western Michigan University and at Vermont College.

Kristy Eldredge writes for the rock website gloriousnoise.com and about fiction for Smokebox.net. She lives in Brooklyn.

Chad Faries has published poems, essays, photographs, interviews, and creative non-fiction in *Mudfish, New American Writing, Barrow Street, The Cream City Review, Afterimage, Post Road*, and others. He has a PhD in Creative Writing from the University of Wisconsin-Milwaukee and was a Fulbright Fellow in Budapest. When not traveling he is a carpenter.

Mark Halliday teaches at Ohio University. He has published four books of poems, including *JAB*, which came out in 2002, published by University of Chicago Press. He received the Rome Prize in Literature from the American Academy of Arts and Letters in 2001.

Judith Hall's *To Put the Mouth To* was selected for The National Poetry Series and published in 1992. Her book, *Anatomy, Errata*, was the winner of the 1997 Ohio State University Press/ The Journal Award in Poetry. Her book of poetry, *The Promised Folly*, appeared in 2003 (TriQuarterly Books/ Northwestern University Press). She serves as poetry editor of *The Antioch Review*.

Forrest Hamer is the author of two books of poetry: *Call & Response* (1995) and *Middle Ear* (2000).

Terrance Hayes is the author of two books of poems, *Hip Logic* (Penguin, 2002) and *Muscular Music* (1999). He has received a Whiting Writers Award and a Kate Tufts Discovery Award for his poetry.

Brian Henry lives in Athens, Georgia. The piece in this issue is the title series for his new book.

Bob Hicok is the author of three collections of poems. His poems have appeared in *The New Yorker, Ploughshares*, and *Poetry*, as well as twice appearing in the *Best American Poetry* and *Pushcart* anthologies. His most recent book, *Animal Soul*, was a finalist for the National Book Critics Circle Award. His fourth book, *Insomnia*

Diary, is forthcoming from University of Pittsburgh Press in 2004. He recently joined the MFA faculty at Virginia Tech.

Amy Holman is a poet and fiction writer living in New York City. She teaches writers how to match up their style of writing to publishers in the marketplace. Her poetry appears in print and online journals, such as *Literal Latte*, *CrossConnect*, *Web Del Sol*, and *Rattapallax*, and in the anthologies *Mercy of Tides: Poems for A Beach House*, *And We the Creatures* and *Best American Poetry 1999*. She has a story in *Night Train*.

Samantha Hunt is an artist and a writer.

Christopher Kennedy is the author of *Nietzsche's Horse* (2001), published by Mitki/Mitki Press.

Ted Kooser has published eight books of poetry, including *Winter Morning Walks: One Hundred Postcards to Jim Harrison* (Carnegie-Mellon Series). He lives on acreage near the village of Garland, Nebraska.

Jaimee Kuperman graduated with her MFA from University of Massachusetts, Amherst. Her poems have appeared in magazines such as *Calyx* and *Patterson Literary Review*.

Patrick Lawler is the author of two books of poems, *A Drowning Man is Never Tall Enough* (The University of Georgia Press, 1990) and *(reading a burning book)* (BASFAL Books, 1994).

Louise Mathias has had poems recently published in *Hunger Mountain*, *Epoch*, *The Journal*, and *Salt Hill Review*, among many other places. She lives in California.

Gretchen Mattox's book, *Goodnight Architecture*, was published by New Issues Press in 2002. She is a co-winner of the 2003 Green Rose Prize for her forthcoming second collection, *Buddha Box*.

Cuban-born **Pablo Medina** is the author of several works of poetry and prose. His most recent collection is *Puntos de apoyo* (poems in Spanish). His collection, *Points of Balance*, is forthcoming from Four Way Books. He teaches at New School University and at the Warren Wilson MFA Program for Writers.

Lydia Melvin is currently a Jay C. and Ruth Halls Poetry Fellow at the University of Wisconsin-Madison. Her poems, to her mother's dismay, have appeared or are forthcoming in *Full Circle*, *Many Mountains Moving*, and *Prairie Schooner*.

Donna Munro is a poet-painter handing out skates and watching the ice in Grand Rapids, Michigan.

William Olsen's third book of poetry, *Trouble Lights*, was brought out by *Triquarterly* in 2002. Along with Sharon Bryan he edited *Planet on the Table, Poets on the Reading Life* (Sarabande, 2003). He teaches at Western Michigan University and Vermont College.

Dzvinia Orlowsky is the author of three books of poems, including *Edge of House* (1999) and *Except for One Obscene Brushstroke* (2002), both published by Carnegie Mellon.

Kevin Prufer's most recent book is *The Finger Bone* (Carnegie Mellon, 2002). He is also editor of *Pleiades: A Journal of New Writing*. New poems are in *Ploughshares, Verse, Epoch, Boulevard, The 2002 & 2004 Pushcart Prize Anthology* and *Best American Poetry 2003*. His new book, *Fallen from a Chariot*, will appear in 2005 from Carnegie Mellon.

Jonathan Pugh comes from South Wales. A former fellow of the Fine Arts Work Center in Provincetown, Massachusetts, he is currently an editor at New Issues Press. He lives in Kalamazoo, Michigan.

Ron Rash is the author of the novel *One Foot in Eden*. His other published works include three books of poetry, two collections of short stories, and a children's book. In 1994 he was awarded an NEA fellowship.

David Rivard's latest books of poems are *Bewitched Playground*, and *Wise Poison*, both published by Graywolf Press.

Dana Roeser's first book of poems, *Beautiful Motion*, is currently seeking a publisher. Her work has appeared in *The Iowa Review, The Laurel Review, The Massachusetts Review, Pool, The Virginia Quarterly Review*, and others.

Mary Ruefle is the author of seven poetry collections, including *Cold Pluto* and *Among the Musk Ox People*, both published by Carnegie Mellon.

Catherine Sasanov's *All the Blood Tethers* was recently released from Northeastern University Press. She is also the author of *Traditions of Bread and Violence* (Four Way Books) and the libretto for *Las Horas de Belén: A Book of Hours*, a theater piece commissioned by Mabou Mines. She lives in Cambridge, Massachusetts.

Christine Schutt lives and teaches in New York City. *Florida*, a novel, will appear in fall, 2003, and *A Day, A Night, Another Day, Summer*, a second collection of stories, in spring 2004, both from Northwestern University Press.

Hugh Seidman's first book, *Collecting Evidence*, won the Yale Series of Younger Poets prize. His *Selected Poems* was published in 1995 by Miami University Press.

Elizabeth Skurnick has been awarded residencies at Yaddo, the VCCA, Sewanee, and the AWP in Prague. Her work has been published by many magazines, including *The Ledge* and *The Delta Review*. She lives in Baltimore.

Maura Stanton has published four books of poetry, a novel, *Molly Companion*, and three collections of short fiction, *The Country I Come From, Do Not Forsake Me, Oh My Darling*, and *Cities in the Sea*. She teaches in the M.F.A. program at Indiana University in Bloomington.

Thomas Swiss teaches at the University of Iowa, where he is editor of the *Iowa Review Web*—a journal of new media, writing and art. He's the author of *Rough Cut* (University of Illinois) and *Measure* (University of Alabama), and the editor of *Mapping the Beat: Popular Music and Contemporary Theory* (Blackwell).

J. C. Todd has poems in *APR, Paris Review, Prairie Schooner* and other journals, as well as two chapbooks, *Nightshade* and *Entering Pisces*. Her column on language and poetry appears in *The Drunken Boat*, where she is a contributing editor. In 2002 she was a VCCA international exchange fellow to Schloss Wiepersdorf, an artists' colony in Germany. She lives in Philadelphia.

Robert VanderMolen's previous collections include *Circumstances* (Sumac Press) and *Breath* (New Issues Press). He was awarded an NEA Fellowship in 1995. He lives in Grand Rapids, Michigan.

Karen Whalley's poems have appeared in *Harvard Review, Passages North*, and *Seattle Review*, and she was the 2001 recipient of the Rona Jaffe Award for women poets. She currently works as a writer for the Department of Community Development for Clallam County and lives in Port Angeles, Washington. Her first book, *The Rented Violin*, is forthcoming from Ausable Press.

Diane Williams's recent book is *Romance Erector*. She is the founder and editor of the literary annual, *NOON*.

Edra Ziesk's second novel, *A Cold Spring*, was published by Algonquin in 2002; her first, *Acceptable Losses*, came out in 1997. She has published short fiction in many journals and quarterlies.